The Complete Guide to Boston's

Freedom Trail

Fourth Edition
by Charles Bahne

The *original* step-by step guidebook
to the walking tour of Boston's historic sites

*Dedicated to
Samuel Adams*

*He organized the Revolution
and helped make this book possible.*

Newtowne Publishing
P. O. Box 381882
Cambridge, Massachusetts 02238-1882
newtownepub@yahoo.com

ISBN 978-0-9615705-3-8

For additional copies of this book, send a check for $8.95 to the address above.
(Massachusetts residents add 56¢ sales tax.)
Quantity purchases are available at a substantial discount — please inquire.

Boston — Then and Now

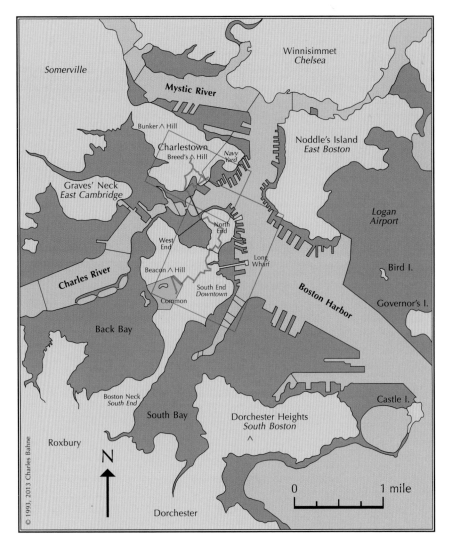

Somerville

Winnisimmet
Chelsea

Mystic River

Bunker ∧ Hill

Charlestown
Breed's ∧ Hill   Navy Yard

Noddle's Island
East Boston

Graves' Neck
East Cambridge

Logan
Airport

North End

West End

Long Wharf

Bird I.

Beacon ∧ Hill

Charles River

South End
Downtown

Common

Boston Harbor

Governor's I.

Back Bay

Boston Neck
South End

South Bay

Dorchester Heights
South Boston
∧

Castle I.

Roxbury

N

0   1 mile

Dorchester

© 1993, 2013 Charles Bahne

Land areas filled in since 1775

Area of detailed maps in this book

Modern place names (where different) are in italics.

The Cradle of Liberty… the birthplace of American Independence… Paul Revere's home and the Old North Church where his lanterns were hung: the very places where our nation began. All of these sites and more can be visited along Boston's Freedom Trail. Here were the gathering places of the patriots, the incubators of revolution… the buildings where American resistance to the British Crown was born, grew, and flourished… until, eventually, the only alternative was war and independence.

The Freedom Trail is a **red line marked on the sidewalk**. It begins at Boston Common and ends at Bunker Hill in Charlestown. Following the Trail is easy — just keep an eye out for the red line. In most places it's made of red bricks set right in the sidewalk pavement, but sometimes the line is painted. Signs also help mark the way from site to site.

From the Common to Copp's Hill — the Boston portion of the Trail — is less than two miles. You can walk it leisurely in under an hour. But an hour will not allow you time to actually visit the historic buildings, burying grounds, and other sites along the Trail. Counting time for lunch, you may want to allow the better part of a day.

The Charlestown section of the Trail can either be done separately or in conjunction with the Boston portion. It's a 20-minute walk, about a mile, from Copp's Hill in the North End to the Navy Yard in Charlestown. Allow at least an hour and a half in Charlestown; more in busy times — in spring and summer — when long lines form to board the *Constitution*. If you want to see everything Charlestown has to offer, you could spend almost a whole day here, too.

In planning your visit, first decide how much time you want to allow — half a day, a full day, or even part of a second day — and then consider following one of the itineraries suggested on the next page.

Keep in mind, too, that the Freedom Trail is a walking tour. ***Don't attempt to drive the Trail!*** Boston's crooked and narrow streets, the utter lack of on-street parking, and the city's many one-way thoroughfares will only lead you to total frustration.

Basic information

☛ **Suggested itineraries:** Depending on how much time you have, consider one of these options for exploring the Trail:

Just part of a day: Take half a day to walk the Trail from Boston Common to the Old North Church, perhaps going into just one site, such as Old South Meeting-House, the Old State House, the Paul Revere House, or Old North Church. If you have a little more time, make brief visits into two or three sites.

A full day on the Trail, from end to end: Devote the morning and early afternoon to a quick exploration of the Boston sites, as above; then, after lunch, continue across the river to Charlestown to see U.S.S. *Constitution* and Bunker Hill.

One day in depth, downtown Boston and the North End only: Spend a leisurely day walking the Trail from the Common to Old North Church and Copp's Hill, taking time to go inside most of the churches, museums, and houses along the way; but omitting Charlestown. You'll see the sites that focus on the beginnings of the American Revolution, but you'll miss *Constitution* and Bunker Hill.

Add part of a second day: Allow a full day to browse through the Boston sites, then follow up on another day with Charlestown, and perhaps also the Tea Party Ships. Consider taking a trolley tour to get around the city on the second day.

☛ **Getting to the Freedom Trail:** The best way to reach the Freedom Trail is Boston's subway system, the T. Park Street station, on the Red and Green Lines, is at the Trail's start on Boston Common. State (Blue/Orange Lines) and Government Center (Green/Blue Lines) are near Faneuil Hall; Haymarket (Green/Orange Lines) is close to the North End. *(For directions to Charlestown, see page 61.)*

If you must drive into town, convenient garages include the Boston Common Garage on Charles Street, and the Government Center Garage at Haymarket Square, near I-93 at the corner of Congress and New Chardon Streets.

☛ **Information centers:** The Freedom Trail starts at the city's official Visitors Information Center on Boston Common, which is operated by the Greater Boston Convention and Visitors Bureau (617-536-4100). The National Park Service has two Visitor Centers: one in Faneuil Hall's first floor (617-242-5642), and another in the Navy Yard next to U.S.S. *Constitution* (617-242-5601).

☛ **National Park:** Seven Freedom Trail sites are part of the **Boston National Historical Park**. Faneuil Hall, Bunker Hill, and the Charlestown Navy Yard are operated by the National Park Service; the other sites are still managed by local historical organizations, which first preserved them many years ago.

☛ **Hours:** From April to October, most major Freedom Trail sites are open seven days a week, 9:30 AM to 5:00 PM. But hours vary by site and you should check the table on page 81 for specific hours. Note that U.S.S. *Constitution* is closed Mondays in summer, and closed on Mondays and Tuesdays in winter.

☛ **Guided walking tours:** In peak season, the National Park Service offers free Ranger-guided tours, featuring several Freedom Trail sites; call 617-242-5642 for info. Several other organizations offer escorted tours covering parts of the Trail for a fee; many of these start at the Visitors Information Center on Boston Common.

☛ **Groups:** Groups wishing to go into the historic sites should make advance reservations with the sites. Often this will allow you to receive special programs and/or group admission discounts. Reservations must be made with each individual site; there is no central office. Phone numbers are listed on page 81.

☞ **Trolley tours:** Boston's narrow by-ways keep tourist trolleys several blocks away from many of the most important historic sites; *you cannot see Paul Revere's house or the Old North Church from any trolley or bus.* But a trolley tour can be quite helpful in getting to Charlestown or the Tea Party Ships, especially if you take part of a second day to visit those sites.

☞ **Restrooms:** Public restrooms are available at the Boston Common Visitors Center, at Faneuil Hall and Quincy Market, at the Navy Yard, and at Bunker Hill. Some Trail sites have restrooms for visitors who pay museum admission. *Plan ahead! "Free" public restrooms are scarce along the Freedom Trail, especially in the North End.*

☞ **Restaurants:** Faneuil Hall Market (also known as "Quincy Market") offers a wide variety of sit-down and take-out restaurants, and the Italian North End has many places to eat. In Charlestown, restaurants are located in City Square; in the Navy Yard; and along Main Street. Fast-food hamburger chains have outlets across from Boston Common, and on Washington Street opposite the Old South.

Boston's oldest restaurant, the **Union Oyster House**, is described on page 38. Charlestown's historic **Warren Tavern** is described on pages 76–77.

☞ **Other concerns:** As in any city, be careful about how and where you display jewelry, cameras, and other valuables. One of Boston's biggest crime problems is theft from parked cars, especially those parked in tourist areas. *Don't leave luggage or other valuables visible, and don't park vans or campers in unguarded areas.*

Why the Revolution? Why Boston?

Many years after the American Revolution, Levi Preston, a member of the Danvers militia, was asked why he had marched to fight on the day of Lexington and Concord. Was it the Stamp Act? The tea-tax? "Intolerable oppressions"? No, no, none of that. "Young man," Preston said, "what we meant in going for those red-coats was this: We had always governed ourselves, and we always meant to. They didn't mean we should."

That, in a nutshell, was the essence of the Revolution.

By 1775, Massachusetts residents had been governing themselves for nearly a century and a half. The citizens of Boston had substantially more liberties than their counterparts in London. Political lifestyles had grown so far apart that people on opposite sides of the Atlantic were, in effect, speaking different languages.

It all goes back to the Puritans, who arrived on these shores in 1630 seeking religious liberty. Wealthier and more literate than colonists elsewhere, they set up a participatory self-government that was unique in the western world. Owing no debts to anyone, they ran their own affairs.

After half a century, King James II tried to take away these privileges, but to little avail. The king's hand-picked governor was soon forced to resign, and most — but not all — of the lost liberties were restored.

In the mid-1700s, the Seven Years' War with France — known here as the French and Indian War — severely drained the royal treasury, and the authorities in London sought to raise revenue from the colonies. Bostonians balked at paying taxation without representation. In the "birth of American independence," James Otis argued most eloquently for colonists' rights at the Old State House in 1761.

With the passage of the Stamp Act, the reaction here turned from gentlemanly speeches to violent protest. When the riots continued in 1768, the Crown sent troops to Boston to restore order.

Seventeen months after the soldiers landed on Long Wharf, tensions between the troops and the citizenry reached the breaking point. Five civilians were slain by British bullets in the "Bloody Massacre" in King Street, March 5, 1770. The troops were removed, and relative calm restored — until the taxation issue was raised again, this time on tea, in 1773.

The protest over the tea was costly. The East India Company's destroyed cargo was valued at 45 times the price of Paul Revere's seven-room house. Parliament retaliated by taking away Boston's self-government and even its livelihood, the port. The troops returned, and soon colonists began to prepare for the inevitable war.

It began at Lexington and Concord, April 19, 1775.

For nearly a year afterwards, Boston was in a state of siege. British troops occupied the capital, while Americans held all the surrounding territory. The Battle of Bunker Hill showed that neither side could profitably attack the other. This stalemate lasted until winter, when Henry Knox sledged in cannon that had been captured earlier at Fort Ticonderoga, New York. Placed atop Dorchester Heights and aimed down at Boston, these artillery pieces left the British Army with no choice but to leave.

On March 17, 1776 — yes, it was St. Patrick's Day — the British presence in Boston ended after 145 years. General Washington had won his first victory.

Three and a half months later, the Declaration of Independence was adopted by the Continental Congress in Philadelphia. When the news reached here, Bostonians celebrated in jubilation.

It had been fifteen years since James Otis' first courtroom speech against the writs of assistance, fifteen long years since their protests had begun.

NEW ENGLAND FLAG.

Chronology

1630 — Puritans arrive in Massachusetts and settle Boston.

1686 — King James II revokes the Massachusetts Bay Colony's charter and installs Sir Edmund Andros as governor.

1689 — Bostonians force Governor Andros to resign.

1756–1763 — Seven Years' War (French and Indian War) drains the British treasury.

1760 — King George III accedes to the British throne.

1761 — James Otis argues against the Writs of Assistance in a court trial at the Old State House.

1763 — Faneuil Hall is dedicated to the "Cause of Liberty" by Otis.

1765 — ***Stamp Act*** passed; riots occur in Boston and other cities.

1766 — Stamp Act repealed; great celebrations.

1767 — ***Townshend Acts*** passed; non-importation boycott begins.

1768 — *June 10,* John Hancock's ship *Liberty* is seized in a disagreement over the payment of customs duties; protesters riot in Boston.

— *October 1,* British troops land in Boston to maintain order.

1770 — *March 5,* **the Boston Massacre**.

1772 — Committees of Correspondence formed to oppose "despotism" of Governor Hutchinson in a dispute over his salary.

1773 — Tea Act passed; *December 16,* **Boston Tea Party**.

1774 — *"Intolerable Acts"*, passed to punish Boston for the destroyed tea, close the town's port and abolish all elected, popular government.

— General Thomas Gage appointed governor by King George III.

— Patriots "practise the military art" and organize the Minute Men.

— *September,* First Continental Congress meets in Philadelphia.

1775 — *April 19,* **Lexington and Concord**. British troops march to Concord to seize "rebel" supplies. Alarmed by Paul Revere and William Dawes, the Minute Men stand on Lexington Green. At daybreak the first shots of the war are fired. **Siege of Boston** begins.

— *June 17,* **Battle of Bunker Hill**. Americans fortify Charlestown, overlooking Boston from the north. British troops suffer over 1,000 casualties as they take the Americans' fort.

— *July 2,* General George Washington arrives at Cambridge to take command of the Continental Army.

1776 — *March 4–5,* Americans fortify Dorchester Heights, overlooking Boston from the south.

— *March 17,* **Evacuation Day**. British troops, government officials, and loyalists sail out of Boston Harbor, never to return.

— *July 4,* Declaration of Independence adopted at Philadelphia.

1781 — Battle of Yorktown (Virginia); final surrender of the British Army.

1783 — Peace treaty is signed between United States and Great Britain.

*Start your tour of the Freedom Trail at the **Visitors Information Center** on Boston Common, near the corner of Tremont and West Streets — about 400 feet south of the Park Street subway station.*

Boston Common

America's oldest public park

The Freedom Trail begins at these 44 acres of open land in the middle of the city, land that has never been built upon. This was once the pasture of Boston's first white settler, William Blackstone. Blackstone came to the New World with a group of early colonists in 1622. When that settlement, about 15 miles south of here, failed, Blackstone moved north to what the Indians called **Shawmut**, or "living waters". For five years he lived here as a hermit, accompanied only by his library of 200 books.

When the Puritans arrived in 1630, they first settled in Charlestown, across the river from Blackstone's cottage. But when their water supply proved inadequate, Blackstone "Came and Acquainted the Governor of an Excellent Spring there [at Shawmut], withal Inviting Him and Soliciting Him Thither."

Thus the Puritans moved across the river, and, on September 7, 1630, they renamed Shawmut **"Boston"** — after a town in England from which many of them had come.

For his generosity, the Puritans gave William Blackstone fifty acres of his own land — three years later.

Blackstone, used to living alone, soon regretted his offer of hospitality. In 1634 he moved to Rhode Island, and sold his pasture here to the townspeople for £30. He returned 25 years later, astride a white bull, to court and marry a local widow.

Blackstone's pasture became the **"Common land"**, or "Common" for short. For many years it was a "trayning field" for the militia, "used for that purpose and for the

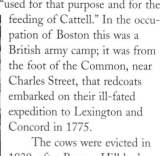

feeding of Cattell." In the occupation of Boston this was a British army camp; it was from the foot of the Common, near Charles Street, that redcoats embarked on their ill-fated expedition to Lexington and Concord in 1775.

The cows were evicted in 1830, after Beacon Hill had become a fashionable residential

area. By that time several "dangerous accidents" had occurred, and, besides, what wealthy Bostonian wanted to have cattle grazing in his front yard?

Also on the Common were the town gallows, where pirates, witches, and heretics — including Quakers — all met their untimely ends.

But the Common is best known as a place for public celebration and demonstration. The 1766 repeal of the Stamp Act brought great rejoicing to this plot of land; in our own time, thousands gathered here to hear Rev. Martin Luther King and again to hear Mass from Pope John Paul II. Sarah Palin spoke here in 2010; every fall an annual "Freedom Rally" promotes the legalization of marijuana.

Any amateur orator is assured an audience on the Common, no matter how strange his or her views may seem. In 1851, for example, passersby were astounded to see a woman wearing pantaloon-like garments, and extolling the virtues of such attire for women. Her name? Amelia Bloomer.

From the Visitors Center, follow the red line down Tremont Street; then bear left and walk uphill towards the golden dome of the State House. On your right will be the Brewer Fountain, imported from Paris in 1867. The Frog Pond, to your left, is a remnant of the city's ancient topography that still provides recreation for summer waders and winter skaters. The frogs, however, are long gone.

Climb the stairs, and look across the street to the State House.

Massachusetts State House

"The Hub of the Solar System" — *Oliver Wendell Holmes*

Construction of Massachusetts' "new" State House was begun in 1795. Fifteen white horses, one for each state in the Union, pulled the cornerstone up the hill, where Samuel Adams (then governor) and Paul Revere presided over its laying.

Three years later the building was completed. Its cost is unclear in the records, but it was several times more than the sum originally budgeted. (Some things never change.) Yet it was acclaimed as the most beautiful and most prominent public building in the still-young nation.

The State House was designed by **Charles Bulfinch**, a Bostonian who took up architecture after visiting England. The success of this project made Bulfinch the leading architect of his day. He also designed state capitols for Connecticut and Maine, and worked on the U. S. Capitol in Washington.

The Bulfinch front, the red brick part of the building, is just 61 feet deep. Everything else has been added since 1895. The dome, long one of the city's chief landmarks, was originally covered with wooden shingles — which leaked. In 1802 it was clad in copper by Paul Revere's firm. This was painted stone gray for many years, and first gilded after the Civil War.

At the top of the grand staircase, the center entrance doors are reserved for visiting presidents, for soldiers returning from war, and for the departing governor at the end of his term.

This, by the way, is still called the "new" State House, to distinguish it from the "Old State House" which still stands on State Street. Only in Boston would a "new" building be more than two centuries old!

The State House is open to the public on weekdays. The entrance is to the right of the main stairs, by the equestrian statue of General Joseph Hooker, who served in the Civil War. To enter, you must pass through a security checkpoint. Guided tours are offered, or you can ask inside for a self-guided tour brochure.

One of the more unusual sights inside the State House is the **"Sacred Cod"**, a life-size carved wooden codfish which hangs in the House of Representatives' chamber. It was first installed in the Old State House in 1784 as "a memorial of the importance of the Cod Fishery to the welfare of the Commonwealth." When Davy Crockett saw it on a visit to Boston, he remarked that he kept antlers and bearpaws in his own house for the same reason.

The State House stands on land once owned by **John Hancock**, the wealthiest merchant in colonial Boston, who was the "milch cow" who funded the secret activities of the Sons of Liberty. Hancock was the first person to sign the Declaration of Independence. He later served as the first elected governor of the Commonwealth of Massachusetts.

Hancock's elegant mansion stood on what is now the west lawn of the State House. Hancock wished to give his home to the state, for use as a governor's mansion, but he died before he could sign his will. Years later, his heirs offered to sell the old house to the state, but the price was considered too high. Much to the dismay of all Bostonians, the Hancock mansion was demolished in 1863.

Beacon Hill

Next to the State House is the fashionable Beacon Hill neighborhood. This, the tallest of Boston's three original hills, was named after the **"beacon"** or alarm signal that was placed atop it in 1634. The beacon was a tall wooden pole with an iron skillet full of pitch at its top. Should the town be attacked, someone would climb the pole and set the pitch afire, a visible call for help from the nearby countryside.

A replacement beacon was erected by the Sons of Liberty in 1768. Neither one was ever used.

When the State House was built, this area was considered remote and "out of town"; only five houses, including Hancock's, stood on the hill. Construction of the

State House made Beacon Hill far more attractive for residences. The top 60 feet of the hill was carted off to fill in the Mill Pond, and within 15 years it was written that "the whole of Beacon Hill, formerly so high, rough, broken & barren, as to render it improbable that it could ever serve for building Lotts, is now almost covered with grand and lofty dwelling houses." Several of these were designed by Charles Bulfinch.

Today Beacon Hill remains the city's finest residential quarter. Chestnut and Mount Vernon streets are the epitome of the Proper Bostonian's Boston, and well worth a few minutes' stroll.

The north side or "back" of the hill was the center of Boston's large African-American community in the early 1800s. Many of the north slope's residents — blacks and whites alike — were active abolitionists, and some houses were stops on the Underground Railroad. Today the back of the hill is the site of the **Black Heritage Trail**, a self-guided tour like the Freedom Trail. You can pick up a free guide to the trail at any of the city's tourist information centers. Included in the trail are the Museum of African American History and the African Meeting House of 1806, the oldest church building erected by free blacks in America.

BEACON.

If you visited the State House or Beacon Hill, cross back to the south side of Beacon Street, next to Boston Common.

But before you walk back down the steps into the park, pause for a moment at the monument which is located between two ancient elm trees, just opposite the State House.

Shaw/54th Regiment Memorial

Directly opposite the State House, facing Beacon Street, stands one of the nation's most important war monuments — a memorial to interracial coöperation as well as to individual heroism.

When the Civil War broke out in 1861, many of Massachusetts' black residents wanted to join in the fight to free their enslaved brethren. But U. S. Army policy prohibited blacks from enlisting.

After pleas from Governor Andrew, the War Department relented and allowed blacks to serve — but not as officers. Some of the state's most prominent young white men then volunteered to lead the black troops of the 54th Massachusetts Regiment. Among these was **Robert Gould Shaw**, only son of one of Boston's first families, and the colonel of the regiment.

It was a risky venture for both black soldier and white officer. The black men, if captured, would become slaves; the whites were seen as traitors to their race by the Confederate Army.

Shaw and 32 of his men were slain leading the assault on Fort Wagner, outside of Charleston, S. C., and were buried in a mass grave at the fort.

This monument was created by **Augustus Saint-Gaudens**, the leading American sculptor of the time. It took 14 years to complete, and was the first sympathetic portrayal of black men by a white artist. Dedicated on Decoration Day of 1897, it is one of the finest works of art to come out of any American war. It's also the starting point for the Black Heritage Trail.

Descend the steps into the Common again. This time, keep to the left, alongside the iron fence, and follow the Freedom Trail's red line towards the white steeple of Park Street Church. At the bottom of the hill, turn left on Tremont Street; pause after you cross Park Street.

Park Street Church

"Brimstone Corner"

Built in 1809, Park Street Church is one of the city's most beautiful landmarks. Henry James termed it "the most interesting mass of bricks and mortar" in America.

The church was designed by Peter Banner, an Englishman who came to America to practice architecture. Solomon Willard, architect of the Bunker Hill Monument, carved the wooden column capitals.

On this site in the 1700s was the town **granary**, with a capacity of over 12,000 bushels. Wheat and other grains were stored here by the town and sold to the needy for a low price. After the Revolution, this practice was ended and the building leased out. In 1797, sails for U.S.S. *Constitution* were made in the loft-like granary.

Shortly after the new State House was completed, the granary was removed, and plans for this building were drawn up, since a church was considered a better-suited neighbor for the state government than a barn.

In its early years, Park Street Church acquired the nickname "Brimstone Corner". This was not for the fire-and-brimstone fervor of the sermons; rather, gunpowder was stored in the crypt during the War of 1812. (Brimstone, or sulfur, is a key ingredient of gunpowder.) Passersby may have been less afraid of eternal hellfire than of the church blowing up!

As an evangelical Christian parish, Park Street has a long tradition of missionary and social work. Here were founded America's first Sunday School

(1817), the first prison aid society (1824), and one of the earliest temperance societies (1826). From this church also were sent the very first missionaries to Hawaii in 1819.

On July 4, 1829, William Lloyd Garrison gave his first public anti-slavery address here. "I will be heard," he said, and eventually he was — over the violent opposition of many Bostonians.

Two years after Garrison's speech, on another Fourth of July, the hymn "America" — also known as "My Country 'tis of Thee" — was sung publicly for the first time on the steps of Park Street. The words were written by Samuel Francis Smith, a divinity student; the tune, a "lilting air" of German origin, is also used in the British anthem "God Save the King".

Immediately beyond Park Street Church, fronting on Tremont Street, is the Granary Burying Ground.

Granary Burying Ground

Last resting place of the Patriots

In this two-acre plot are the remains of more famous people than any other small graveyard in America. Within its bounds lie buried three signers of the Declaration of Independence, nine governors of Massachusetts, the five victims of the Boston Massacre, Benjamin Franklin's parents, and, yes, Paul Revere. Even a Mother Goose is interred in the Granary.

This is the city's third oldest burying place, first used in 1660. It was originally part of the Common, and its name derives from the old grain warehouse that once stood next door on the site of Park Street Church.

Before you enter the graveyard, pause on the sidewalk near the church, and look through the fence. Here a boulder commemorates **James Otis**, whose 1761 speech against the writs of assistance was "the birth of the child Independence". Otis was the patriots' spiritual leader until he was clubbed over the head by a British officer in a barroom brawl. Then he rapidly lost his sanity and became more of an embarrassment than a hero.

Go in the granite entrance gate and climb the steps into the burying ground.

Almost in the exact center of the graveyard is the **Franklin cenotaph**, marking the grave of Benjamin's parents, Josiah and Abiah. (Ben is buried in Philadelphia, where he lived most of his adult life.) The stone obelisk was erected by a group of citizens in 1827, to replace an earlier marker. The laudatory inscription is from the pen of "their youngest son", none other than Ben Franklin himself.

Near the monument are two original gravestones for other members of the Franklin family. Another ancient stone, marking the grave of Ben's uncle "Benjamen" — after whom the patriot was named — has unfortunately disappeared in recent decades.

As you look around the burial ground you will see **three kinds of graves**. Most common are the ones marked by a **headstone** — and sometimes also by a footstone. As these stones have been rearranged several times over the years, today they bear little relation to the bodies actually buried beneath them. **Table tombs** look just like their name. No one is actually buried above ground; the tables are just permanent markers for the brick-encased tombs below. **Vaults**, another kind of tomb, are found around the perimeter of the burying ground. Markers for these are usually flush in the ground or attached to a nearby wall or fence.

Vaults and table tombs were preferred by wealthy families, since they were more secure and could actually be owned by a family. Each tomb usually has several people buried in it, even though there may be only one name on the tombstone.

From the Franklin monument, take the path to the left, towards Park Street Church; then walk to the right and around the burial ground.

Beside a nearby building, a tall white pillar marks the tomb of **John Hancock**. This stone shaft is a replacement; the original tombstone disappeared over a century ago. It has even been suggested that Hancock's remains may have been lifted by a graverobber, as the tomb lay open for some time while a nearby wall was being rebuilt.

Beside the Hancock monument, next to the path, is a stone to the memory of "**Frank**, Servant to John Hancock Esqr.", who died in 1771 at the age of 38. The absence of a last name on the gravestone likely implies that Frank was Hancock's slave. Slavery was common in pre-Revolutionary Massachusetts, although not on the scale of the large southern plantations. Most northern slaves were household servants or coachmen. Even the fiery patriot Samuel Adams inherited two slaves, from his wife's family.

During the Revolution, local Loyalists fled to Canada and abandoned their slaves here, while slaves of patriot owners often earned freedom by fighting in the war. By 1783 there were so few slaves left in Massachusetts that slavery was abolished, the first state in the Union to do so.

In the left rear corner of the graveyard, near an office building, is the table tomb of **Peter Faneuil**, benefactor of Boston's market and town meeting hall. Faneuil was of French Huguenot (Protestant) descent, and his name was as difficult for 18th-century Bostonians to pronounce as it is for us today. When he died, the stonecutter

carved his name on the tombstone the way it was pronounced: "P. FUNAL". This early inscription has since disappeared; the correct spelling, carved later, is easily legible.

Midway along the rear path, on your left, you will find a square monument of white marble that marks

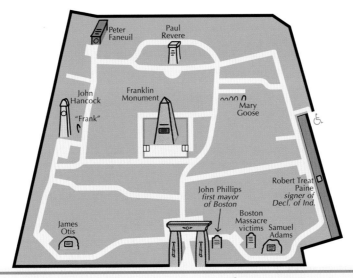

Tremont   Street

the grave of **Paul Revere**, patriot, Son of Liberty, and hero of the famous midnight ride — as well as quite an able craftsman. Revere was already 40 years old that fateful night; he lived another 43 years to 1818.

> *Turn right at the next path and walk back towards the Franklin monument. As you near the first tree on your left, turn onto the second, dead-end path. Near here is buried Boston's "**Mother Goose**".*

Elizabeth Goose, who died in 1757, was the second wife of Isaac Goose. She raised twenty children — ten of her own, and ten by Isaac's first wife, Mary. When Isaac died, Elizabeth moved in with her daughter and fourteen grandchildren, where she lived to the age of 92.

There the facts end, but we can assume that, like any good grandmother, Elizabeth Goose spent many an hour reciting nursery rhymes to the little ones gathered around the fire. Legend has it that her son-in-law, a printer, published a book of these stories titled *Songs for the Nursery, or Mother Goose's Melodies*. The legend remains unproven, for no copies of the book have ever been found.

Regrettably, we must acknowledge that Elizabeth was not the *original* "Mother Goose". There were others before her both in England and in France, and most of the Mother Goose tales go back years before Elizabeth Goose's day. Still, it is comforting to know that there was indeed a real woman named "Mother Goose", who lived in Boston, whether or not she actually wrote any nursery rhymes.

Alas! You won't find Elizabeth's gravestone; that disappeared long ago. But you will see a marker for "yᵉ body of Mary Goose", Isaac's first wife. And if you like, you can tell the little ones with you that here lies Mrs. Goose, an old woman who had so many children she didn't know what to do — so she told them nursery rhymes.

Walk back towards the entrance gate; turn left on the path which parallels the iron fence, until you come to a large granite boulder.

The stone marks the tomb of **Samuel Adams**, the "organizer of the Revolution". It is often said that it was Hancock's money and Adams' brains that fueled the revolt. Adams' fiery writings, combined with his deft political maneuvering, kept public passions aroused for years.

Appropriately next to Adams' grave is that of the five **victims of the Boston Massacre**: Samuel Gray, Samuel Maverick, James Caldwell, Crispus Attucks, and Patrick Carr. Buried with them is Christopher Snider, a young boy killed by a Tory in another incident 11 days earlier. He was the first victim of the struggles between the colonists and the mother country.

Exit the burial ground, and continue along Tremont Street. King's Chapel, the trail's next stop, is half a block ahead on the right.

As you cross Tremont Street towards the stone church, be sure to look down the street to your left (away from Boston Common) for a quick glimpse of the white steeple of the Old North Church in the distance.

King's Chapel

Symbol of what the Puritans fled

In many ways the story of King's Chapel reflects the religious and political history of early Massachusetts.

The Puritans who settled Boston in 1630 were religious rebels fleeing the "heresy", "popery", and corruption they saw in the official Church of England (also called the Anglican Church). Half a century later, King James II ordered the establishment of an Anglican parish in Boston — which was exactly what the Puritans had left England to get away from.

Where to build the new church posed quite a problem, since no Puritan would sell the Anglicans any suitable land. So in 1687 Governor Andros simply seized a corner of the burying ground, assuming rightly that the dead could never complain. One critic called it a "bare-faced squat".

The present structure of rough-dressed granite was begun in 1749. It was erected *around* the earlier wooden chapel, so as not to disturb the weekly services. When the new church was finished, the old one was dismantled, and its pieces tossed out through the windows.

This was the second building designed by **Peter Harrison**, America's first architect. Harrison, who lived in Newport, R. I., worked strictly by mail order. You

sent him a letter stating what you wanted, and he sent back the plans. He never came to Boston.

The simple exterior belies the elegant interior, one of the most beautiful in New England. Local craftsmen lacked tools to carve delicate designs in the hard stone, so the outside was necessarily left plain.

Inside, though, are hand-carved, coupled Corinthian columns and the original box pews with their high walls to conserve body warmth in cold New England winters. The wineglass **pulpit** with its sounding board dates from 1717 and was used in the old wooden chapel. It is the oldest pulpit in continual use on the same site in America.

As King's Chapel was the first and leading Anglican church in New England, it was favored with frequent gifts from British royalty. Several of these are displayed today behind the altar, but the communion silver was carried off to Halifax in 1776 by the rector, Dr. Henry Caner.

Along the right wall is the canopied **Governor's Pew**, used by the royal governors as well as by President Washington on his 1789 visit to Boston. The pew was dismantled in 1826 as an "undemocratic reminder of another era"; it was restored early in the 20th century.

In the gallery at the rear of the church, you can see the organ, a replica of the original 1713 instrument. This was the first organ to be permanently installed in any church in British America.

To many Bostonians, the organ and other elegant trappings were symbols of the British churches from which their ancestors had fled. Even more suspicious was the congregation's mounting political power. Royal governors, colonial officials, and hated army and navy officers all worshipped here at King's Chapel.

To arouse further indignation, rector Caner openly advocated the establishment of a Boston bishop. This was seen by the Puritans' descendants as a direct threat to their own freedom of religion. In Britain, church and nobility were enmeshed in corrupt politics; Bostonians wanted no part of that.

So when the cornerstone for this new King's Chapel was laid in 1749, angry citizens threw garbage, dead animals, and curses at the celebrants.

Hostility towards King's Chapel remained high until the Revolution. When the British Army evacuated Boston in 1776, nearly half the pewholders left with them. For years afterwards, the building was known as "Stone Chapel".

In 1785 the remaining congregation, led by pastor James Freeman, adopted a new theology and became the first Unitarian church in America. Today the parish still follows a unique combination of Unitarian beliefs with liturgy adapted from the Anglican *Book of Common Prayer*.

Outside the chapel, look carefully at the **columns** of the front portico. They are not made of stone, but of wood, with sand mixed into the paint to resemble stone. Although part of Peter Harrison's original design, the portico was not built until 40 years later for lack of funds. A steeple was likewise planned, but never built.

Continue past the church on Tremont Street, away from Boston Common, to the adjacent burial ground.

King's Chapel Burying Ground

Next door to King's Chapel is Boston's first and oldest burying place, first used just a few months after the town was settled in 1630.

It is often assumed that this burying ground is somehow connected with its neighbor church. As we have seen, however, this is not so; the church was erected over 50 years later on land taken from the burial ground. Here are buried some of Boston's stanchest Puritans, who must surely have spun in their caskets when an Anglican church was built so close to their own tombs!

Just inside the graveyard's gate is one of the most beautiful of all Boston gravestones, the elaborately carved stone of **Joseph Tapping** (d. 1678). Latin inscriptions

— *Fugit hora* ("Time flies"); *Memento mori* ("Remember that you must die") — and the ever-present death's head surround a picture of Father Time snuffing out the candle of Life. The carving was done by a man known only as "the Charlestown stonecutter".

The funereal beauty of Tapping's headstone reminds us that Boston's old graveyards are also galleries of art and literature. If you limit your quest to the tombs of famous people, you will lose much of the pleasure of these old burial grounds. Look also for unusual epitaphs, and for the fine work of 17th- and 18th-century craftsmen.

No one knows how many people are buried here, for accurate records were never kept. For each stone you see, there were probably ten or twenty burials. As early as 1738, Boston's gravediggers complained that "oft times they were obliged to bury the dead four deep." Yet burials here continued for many decades after that!

These colonial graveyards were macabre places indeed, with pieces of caskets and even bones often poking up through the soil. Today they are in better shape, but many of the ancient stones are falling in pieces — the result of natural forces, pollution, carelessness, and outright vandalism. So please be careful as you walk through these burial grounds, and remember that *gravestone rubbing is not allowed.*

In the middle of the burial ground is a cluster of notable graves. Here are **Mary Chilton**, the first Pilgrim to touch land in America, and **William Paddy**, whose 1658 gravestone is the oldest still extant in Boston.

Plaques say that here lies **William Dawes**, the "other man" who rode to Lexington at midnight; but they lie: In 2006, historians discovered documents showing that he was never buried here! His relatives are here, but William is now in an unmarked tomb at Forest Hills Cemetery in Jamaica Plain.

Just to the north of these is the table tomb of John Winthrop, first governor of the Massachusetts Bay Colony, and the guiding light of the early Puritan settlement.

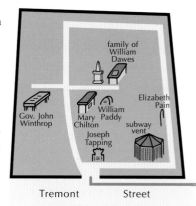

Along the south walk, near the church, is the grave of **Elizabeth Pain**, who may be better known today as "Hester Prynne", the fictional heroine of Nathaniel Hawthorne's novel *The Scarlet Letter*. Hawthorne, who often wandered through this graveyard in the early 1800s, used Elizabeth's headstone as the inspiration for his story. It has been said that there were many similarities between the fictional Hester and the real-life Elizabeth.

The octagonal cage in the burial ground's front corner is not a tomb, but a ventilator shaft for the 1898 subway — America's first — under Tremont Street. Think of it as a monument to Charlie, "the man who never returned" from the Kingston Trio's hit song of the 1950s.

Leaving the burial ground, turn left and retrace your steps past King's Chapel; then turn left again at the corner onto School Street.

Site of the first public school

Just beyond King's Chapel, where the sidewalk widens, is a hopscotch-like mosaic embedded in the pavement. This artwork by Lilli Ann Killen Rosenberg commemorates the original site of **Boston Latin School**.

Reading the Bible was a basic element of the Puritan faith, "it being one chief project of that old deluder, Satan, to keep men from the knowledge of the Scriptures." Thus education — learning to read — was of primary importance. So almost as soon as the colony's survival was assured, the town voted that "our brother Philemon Pormont shall be intreated to become schole-master for the teaching and nourtering of children with us." The date was April 13, 1635.

The school was unique in the world, for children, rich or poor, could attend without paying tuition. Yet there were restrictions. Few poor children attended, since students had to pay for firewood, and families often needed the children to help out with chores around the house, or even to earn a living. And girls and children of color weren't allowed to attend public schools in the colonial era. They were often home-tutored.

For a decade classes were held in the schoolmaster's home. Then in 1645 the first school building was built on this site. This crude wooden

structure was removed a century later, to make way for the enlarged King's Chapel that stands today. Among those who had studied in this first school building were Benjamin Franklin, John Hancock, and Samuel Adams.

Now located in another part of the city, Boston Latin is still the pride of the city's public school system. Admission is by competitive exam, and even today four years of Latin are still required to graduate.

A **statue of Benjamin Franklin**, the Latin School's most famous dropout, stands in the nearby courtyard. A sidewalk café now surrounds Boston's first public portrait statue, erected in 1856. Richard S. Greenough, the sculptor, said that he found "the left side of the great man's face philosophical and reflective and the right side, funny and smiling." And so he claimed to carve it. You may try to see for yourself.

Across the courtyard is a statue of **Josiah Quincy**, Boston's second mayor, and the man responsible for erecting Quincy Market.

Behind the two statues, the "granite granny of School Street" is Boston's **Old City Hall**, erected in 1864 in the fashionable French Second Empire style. Not used by the city since 1968, this "Parisian wedding cake" now houses private offices and a restaurant.

SIDETRIP: You may wish to leave the Freedom Trail for a moment, to view another landmark of old Boston. Cross School Street and walk up Province Street; near the end of the block, you'll come to a flight of stone stairs on your right.

The Province Steps

These unusual granite steps are all that remain of the elegant **Province House**, the official residence of the Massachusetts colony's royal governors. The house itself, which faced Washington Street, burned down 150 years ago. These steps led back from the mansion into its formal gardens.

It was in the Province House that General Gage planned the British march to Lexington and Concord. This was one of the worst-kept secrets in all military history. A groom in the stables overheard some officers talking, and he told their plans to a friend. "There will be hell to pay tomorrow," he said. The second stableboy then went to Paul Revere with the news. "You are the third person who has brought me the same information," commented Revere. Needless to say, there *was* hell to pay — for the British.

END OF SIDETRIP: Return to School Street and resume following the red line. The Trail's next site, the Old Corner Book Store, is at the end of the block on your left.

Old Corner Book Store

"Parnassus Corner"

The small brick house at the corner of School and Washington streets is one of Boston's oldest surviving structures. Erected around 1718 for Thomas Crease, an apothecary, it was his shop, office, and home.

But its greatest fame arose in the mid-1800s, when it was the literary capital of America. From 1833 to 1864, this was the office of **Ticknor and Fields**, the nation's leading book publisher. The greatest authors in American history regularly gathered here: Longfellow, Hawthorne, Emerson, and Harriet Beecher Stowe, among others. The English writers Thackeray and Dickens visited as well.

This was the "flowering of New England", as Van Wyck Brooks put it, an intellectual revolution that echoed the political one of 1776. Boston was "the Athens of America".

From this venerable building were published *Walden*, *The Scarlet Letter*, and *Hiawatha*, as well as Julia Ward Howe's "Battle Hymn of the Republic". So too was the *Atlantic Monthly*, an old Boston institution which thrived in the city for 148 years before moving elsewhere.

No other building in America has been associated with so many great writers and their works. Restored in the 1960s, this literary mecca for many years served as a newspaper office and bookstore. Regrettably, it's now home to a fast-food burrito parlor.

This is only the second building ever to occupy this corner. The first was the home of **Anne Hutchinson**, who was banished from Massachusetts in 1638 for preaching her unorthodox religious views. (Her sin was to believe in a Covenant of *Grace* instead of a Covenant of *Works* — and to challenge the male authorities.) Her house, along with most of this part of town, was destroyed in the Fire of 1711, caused by "a poor Sottish Woman" burning rubbish.

*Turn right on Washington Street, noticing the **Boston Irish Famine Memorial** on the plaza to your right. Old South Meeting-House, with its tall copper steeple, is just across the street on your left.*

Old South Meeting-House

"Nursery and Sanctuary of Freedom"

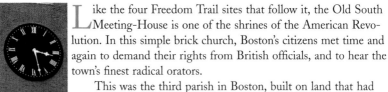

Like the four Freedom Trail sites that follow it, the Old South Meeting-House is one of the shrines of the American Revolution. In this simple brick church, Boston's citizens met time and again to demand their rights from British officials, and to hear the town's finest radical orators.

This was the third parish in Boston, built on land that had once belonged to Governor John Winthrop. The present meeting-house was erected in 1729–30 by Joshua Blanchard, mason, replacing the cedar meeting-house built 60 years earlier. The building is remarkably plain, especially compared to Boston's two other surviving colonial churches. Old South was a Congregational, or "Puritan", parish, whose members shunned ritual and elegance; they thought it more important to hear the sermon than to have elaborate ceremony.

Old South's role in history came about by accident — it was the largest meeting hall in town. When crowded gatherings overflowed Faneuil Hall, they moved here. As tensions escalated, more and more of the crucial events that led up to the Revolution took place at Old South.

One of the earliest of these angry meetings came on the day after the Boston Massacre. Thousands of citizens marched here from Faneuil Hall to demand that all the troops "guarding" their town be removed. "Both regiments or none!" was their cry, and Lt. Gov. Hutchinson had to give in.

After the bloodshed of the Massacre had passed, events in town remained calm for nearly four years. But passage of the **Tea Act** and shipment of a cargo of that "bainfull weed" aroused passions once again.

BOSTON, OLD SOUTH CHURCH WITH NEW OLD SOUTH BUILDING.

Dartmouth, first of the tea ships, entered Boston Harbor on November 28, 1773. By law, the cargo had to be unloaded, and the tax paid, within twenty days.

During the three weeks after *Dartmouth*'s arrival, many meetings were held. But the negotiations were fruitless. Governor Hutchinson would not allow the ship to return to England with its cargo, as the patriots wanted.

The deadline was December 16, at midnight. That day, some 7,000 citizens came to Old South, spilling out into the surrounding streets. A delegation was sent to Governor Hutchinson's country estate with a final plea.

At a quarter to six, the delegation returned. Hutchinson had once again refused.

After a while, Samuel Adams told the crowd, "Gentlemen, this meeting can do nothing more to save the country."

Recent research by historian Ray Raphael has found that Adams was not, in fact, giving a signal, as a century-old legend has claimed. But not long after Adams' words, nearly a hundred men, disguised as Mohawk Indians, appeared outside the meeting-house doors. Amidst war whoops, the cry "To the wharves!" rang out. "Boston Harbour a tea-pot tonight!" The "Indians", followed by over a thousand spectators, rushed down to Griffin's Wharf.

Over a year later, one more momentous meeting was held here at Old South. On March 6, 1775, Dr. Joseph Warren delivered an oration "perpetuating the memory of the horrid massacre" on its fifth anniversary. Again thousands of people packed the meeting-house, so tightly that Warren had to climb in through a window.

Legend has it that a British ensign was planning to throw an egg at Warren at the first sign of treason. In the ensuing confusion, all of the town's leading patriots — including Warren, Adams, and Hancock — were to have been arrested. It was a wonderful plan, except for one thing. The ensign fell on his way to the meeting, breaking his leg (as well as the egg), and he never showed up.

During the siege of Boston, this "sanctuary of freedom" was wantonly dese-crated by His Majesty's troops who were occupying the town. The church was used as a stable and a riding-school, and drinks were served at a bar in the gallery. "The beautiful carved pew of Deacon Hubbard, with the silken hangings, was taken down and carried to ————'s house by an officer and made a hog-stye." The other pews and the pulpit were chopped into firewood, while some of the fine library of Rev. Prince was burned for kindling.

When the British left, Old South was restored and used as a church for nearly a century more. But in 1872 the congregation moved to put up a new Gothic building in Copley Square. The old meeting-house was sold to be torn down, and demolition actually begun. Numerous schemes were offered to save the Old South, including one plan to jack up the historic church and build four stories of offices beneath it!

At the very last moment, Boston's lovers of history — led by a group of women — raised the money to buy the shrine. It was one of the very first buildings in America to be preserved solely for its historical associations. Ever since, the Old South Meeting-House has been open to the public as a museum and a haven for free speech.

Inside, exhibits chronicle the history of Old South, including a book of poems by Phillis Wheatley, America's first published black author, who was a member of the congregation. Museum staff are on hand to tell you more about the controversies that have rung inside these historic walls over the past 280 years.

The exit from Old South is on Milk Street. As you emerge, look up at the building across the street. (If you didn't go inside, walk a few yards up Milk Street — on the right of the meeting-house — and look across to the second, cream-colored building.)

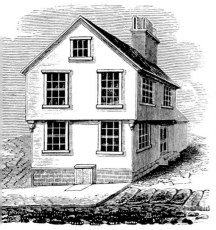

Inscribed on the second-floor façade of the building at 17 Milk Street are the words "**Birthplace of Franklin**", next to a bust of the philosopher and statesman. In a rude, two-story cottage on this site, Benjamin Franklin was born on January 6, 1706. The house burned down in 1810, but a sketch of it survives.

Return now to Washington Street and follow the Freedom Trail's red line north, past Old South's front door.

*Opposite the Old Corner Book Store, look on your right for an alley. This is **Spring Lane**, where the Great Spring furnished much of the town's water for many years. Here too was the 17th-century home of Governor John Winthrop.*

Go past Spring Lane, cross Water Street, and continue down Washington Street for another block, until you come to the Old State House on the right.

The main stem of Boston's street system, **Washington Street** was for a century and a half the only road into or out of town. All commerce had to pass by here, unless it went by boat. This was the route taken by William Dawes on April 18, 1775, while Paul Revere was getting ready to row across the Charles River.

General Washington entered Boston on this street on March 18, 1776, the day after the British troops evacuated the city; his triumphant entrance into town that day marked his first victory of the war.

Thirteen years later, now President, Washington again visited Boston. Almost the entire populace greeted him — except for John Hancock, then governor of Massachusetts, who claimed to be ill. After a tremendous parade, this "highway to Roxbury" was renamed in Washington's honor.

SIDETRIP: You may wish to leave the Trail here to observe another historic site. Walk past the Old State House to the corner of State Street (originally "King Street"). This, the northwest corner of the Old State House, served as Boston's "zero milestone" in colonial days. Washington Mall ("Cornhill") is directly ahead.

*Look to the left up Court Street ("Queen Street"), past the Ames Building with its many granite arches. Just beyond the Shelter for Homeless Veterans is an alley known as **Franklin Avenue**.*

The Veterans' Shelter stands today on the site where James Franklin had his printing shop in the early 1700s. Here James' younger brother Benjamin served his apprenticeship. The teenaged Ben Franklin got his first taste of politics here as well, for his brother's newspaper, the *New England Courant*, was once banned by British authorities for its outspokenness.

From this same printing office a few decades later, **Edes and Gill** published *The Boston Gazette*, one of the most radical of all the town's newspapers. Samuel Adams wrote many a column for the *Gazette*, under such pen names as "Vindex", "Populus", and "a Bostonian".

But this was more than just a newspaper office. The **"long room"** above it was the earliest and most secret meeting place of the patriot plotters. Here Adams and Revere, Otis and Warren, and a very select few others planned their moves.

It is very likely, although we will never know for sure, that some of the plans to destroy the hated tea were made and discussed here at Edes and Gill's.

End of sidetrip: Retrace your steps up Washington Street, to the small pedestrian plaza on the south side of the Old State House (the side closest to Old South).

Old State House

"Here the child Independence was born"

Erected in 1713, the Old State House is the oldest public building still standing in the eastern United States. The tiny "jewel box" at the head of State Street, now dwarfed by skyscrapers, was once the most imposing structure in all Boston.

This was the capitol of the colony, the center of British authority, where the governor and other royally-appointed officials met. But it was also the meeting place of the **Massachusetts Assembly**, freely elected by the people. Inevitably, then, the Old State House became the scene of many a confrontation between the colonists and their royalist rulers.

The "first scene of the first act of opposition" was James Otis' speech against the **writs of assistance**, given in the old Council Chamber in 1761, a full 15 years before independence was declared. Otis' oratory inspired the hearts of all who heard it. John Adams wrote, many years later, that "Otis was a flame of fire. With… a prophetic glance of his eye into futurity, and a torrent of impetuous eloquence, he hurried away everything before him. Every man of a crowded audience appeared to me ready to go away, as I did, ready to take arms…. Then and there the child Independence was born."

But Otis lost his case. The judge, Thomas Hutchinson, held a number of royal posts; in effect, he was judge, jury, and prosecutor all at once. Naturally, he sided with the King.

In the room next to the council chamber met the Assembly, by far the most radical of all the colonial legislatures. In 1766, during the debate on the Stamp Act, the representatives installed a gallery so that the public could sit in on their sessions. This was the first time in modern history that ordinary citizens could

watch their government at work. But "watching" was not the whole purpose. Crowds of patriots often sat in the gallery, heckling and intimidating those members of the Assembly who dared to vote the Tory line.

Naturally, the legislature's outspokenness aroused the ire of the royal authorities. Year after year, the governor refused to allow them to meet, or forced them to convene in distant towns far from Boston's agitators. Important measures were often passed behind locked doors, while outside a royal messenger waited with orders for the Assembly's adjournment.

After the Revolution, Massachusetts' government left the Old State House when the new one on Beacon Hill was completed in 1798. For most of the next century, this structure was rented out for stores and offices.

So disfigured and unrecognizable was the Old State House that in the 1870s the city proposed to tear it down to widen the street. Don't do that, protested some Chicagoans; we'll move it brick by brick to the shores of Lake Michigan, "for all America to revere." Bostonians were so offended by this offer that they decided to preserve and restore this shrine right where it had always stood.

Since 1882, then, the Old State House has been a **museum** operated by the Bostonian Society, with fascinating exhibits about the town's role in the American Revolution. Among the items on display are a replica of the red velvet coat that John Hancock wore to his inauguration as Massachusetts' first elected governor; and a British soldier's gun, found on King Street after the Boston Massacre.

Should you go inside, keep in mind that the building's interior has been altered — several times! — over the years. The gallery and even the Assembly chamber have vanished without a trace; even the striking spiral staircase is a 19th-century addition.

Be sure to look out from the balcony at the end of the second-floor council chamber. At the far end of State Street, you can see the red brick buildings of **Long Wharf** on Boston's waterfront. Built at the same time as the Old State House, Long Wharf was for many years the port's only deep-water pier. The shoreline was then just a block and a half away from the Old State House. As the land beyond has been filled in, Long Wharf has slowly disappeared into the mainland.

The proximity to the wharf made this colonial Boston's business center as well. The town's first **merchant's exchange**, a precursor of the stock exchange, met daily on the Old State House's ground floor. Ever since, State Street has been a financial center, as its many sprouting skyscrapers will attest today.

Leave the Old State House on the opposite side of the building from where you came in, then turn right to rejoin the Trail. If you didn't go inside, follow the Freedom Trail's red line past the entrance, and turn left at the corner.

Pause a moment now to look back at the east façade of the Old State House.

In the building's east gable is a **clock** made by Simon Willard. First installed in 1831, it was covered over some years ago and then revealed during restorations in 1992. A square sundial was once mounted in this spot.

Below the clock is the **balcony** from which the royal governors made their official proclamations to the colony. But the tables were turned on July 18, 1776, when Col. Thomas Crafts stood here and read the Declaration of Independence, a copy of which had arrived from Philadelphia. That night jubilant citizens staged a bonfire in this

square. Consigned to the flames were flags and other reminders of British rule, including the original lion and unicorn — the royal symbols of Great Britain — from atop the Old State House itself.

Today that event is commemorated every year with a Fourth of July reading of the Declaration from the Old State House balcony — but no bonfire.

The present **lion and unicorn**, by the way, are replicas, installed in 1882 when the building was first restored.

The Boston Massacre

A **circle of paving stones** in the walkway below the balcony theoretically marks the site of the "horrid massacre" of March 5, 1770. In the first bloodshed of the American Revolution, five Bostonians were killed when a squad of British officers fired into a taunting, jeering mob.

British troops, called "regulars", landed at Long Wharf and occupied Boston in the fall of 1768 after riots the previous spring. The tensions of a poor economy only heightened citizens' resentment of the redcoats in their midst. A year and a half later, the town was a powderkeg ready to explode.

Trouble began late in February, 1770, when a schoolboy named Christopher Snider was shot and killed by an "abandoned wretch" of a Tory during a mêlée. The boy's funeral, organized by Samuel Adams, drew thousands of angry citizens.

Eight days later, on March 2, a British soldier, seeking a job, was told to "clean my shithouse." Another riot broke out.

On Monday, March 5, rumor had it that there would again be trouble. The town was filled with people, mostly boys and young men, milling about. Many were from out of town. In fact, the Massacre was only one of many arguments and brawls that broke out on Boston streets that day.

This one began innocently enough, with a dispute over a barber bill. A wigmaker's apprentice was pestering an army officer, tailing him all over town, insulting him about the debt — which had, in truth, been paid. Eventually, the officer entered a tavern on King Street, opposite the State House. The apprentice continued his harassment outside. A soldier on guard at the nearby Custom House joined the argument and struck the boy with the barrel of his musket. A crowd started to gather. Then somebody rang a nearby church bell — normally used as a fire alarm — and still more people turned out. Many were armed with sticks and clubs.

At the 29th Regiment's nearby headquarters, Capt. Thomas Preston "walked up and down for near half an hour," wondering what to do. The lone guard, surrounded by dozens of hostile citizens, was clearly in mortal danger.

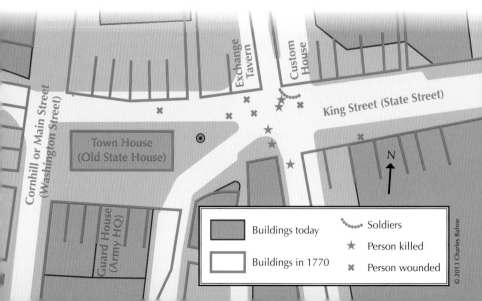

At last Preston led a rescue party to the Custom House to bring the sentry back to safety. But once there, Preston and his eight men were themselves trapped and could not return.

For fifteen minutes the crowd grew uglier, daring the soldiers to fire, cursing them, pressing closer and closer. Snowballs and rocks flew through the night air. Suddenly a thrown club hit one of the redcoats, knocking him down on the ice. He stood up and fired at point-blank range. More shots quickly rang out.

Preston frantically ordered his men to cease fire. But three people lay dead in the street, two others were dying, and several more were wounded.

The slain men were a cross-section of Boston. One, Crispus Attucks, was black; another, Patrick Carr, was Irish-born. Three of the five were young apprentices to local craftsmen.

The patriots played up the incident for all they could. Their perennial villain, Lt. Gov. Hutchinson, was forced to remove the troops to Castle Island in the harbor. Samuel Adams "observed his Knees to tremble" as Hutchinson addressed the crowd. "I thought I saw his face grow pale (and I enjoyed the sight)," wrote Adams.

Paul Revere's famous engraving of the "Bloody Massacre" — shown on the next page — was copied after an illustration by Henry Pelham. Revere's view was factually inaccurate, but it was great propaganda. Prints of it were sold throughout the town and carried all over the colonies as well as back to England.

Boston Massacre Site — Then and Now

The BLOODY MASSACRE perpetrated in King—Street BOSTON on Mar. 5 1770 by a party of the 29th REGT

Engrav'd Printed & Sold by Paul Revere Boston

But Boston was not yet ready for war. With the troops removed, things quieted considerably. Two ardent patriots, John Adams and Josiah Quincy, defended the Massacre soldiers in court and won acquittal for all but two of them. The two guilty men were branded on their thumbs and set free.

First installed in 1887, the memorial **circle of stones** was put in the middle of the street, nearer the site where Crispus Attucks fell. It's been moved at least three times; the present location was chosen merely so that people can safely stand around it, without being hit by traffic. In fact, the Massacre site was spread widely throughout the intersection, as the diagram on the opposite page shows. Free tours of the Massacre site area are included with admission to the Old State House.

Faneuil Hall, the Freedom Trail's next stop, is just half a block away. But before we go there, we'll take a look at what one historian has called a "catalyst for revolution", the single most important event leading up to American independence.

SIDETRIP: Although not an official Freedom Trail site, the **Boston Tea Party** *merits discussion here. Today's Boston Tea Party Ships are anchored at the Congress Street Bridge, six blocks away from here; this is the closest that the Trail comes to them.*

Because of their distance from the Trail, many visitors prefer to visit the ships on a separate day, perhaps as part of a trolley tour. To visit them now, walk south on Congress Street through Boston's financial district. When you get to Atlantic Avenue, cross to the left side of Congress Street and continue south for another block.

Boston Tea Party

"The boldest stroke which had yet been struck in America"
— *Thomas Hutchinson*

More than any other single event in its history, Boston is known for its Tea Party. Neither the Stamp Act Riots, nor the Boston Massacre, nor even Paul Revere's ride, have quite the fame of Samuel Adams' "Indian caper". Mention Boston to a British subject today, for example, and the likely response will be, "Ah, yes, that's where they dumped the bloody tea!" In our own country, 21st-century political groups remind us of the Tea Party's historical significance.

It is fitting, for the Boston Tea Party was the turning point of the protests that led to Revolution. Once tea leaves had mingled with the salt waters of Boston Harbor, things "had gone too far to recede." Even Governor Hutchinson acknowledged that. War — and separation from Britain — was now the only recourse.

Parliament had first levied a tax on tea with the Townshend Acts of 1767. But this law was ineffective. At first, non-importation boycotts prevented taxed tea from being sold; then, smuggled tea from Holland undercut the price of the legal, taxed tea. By 1773 the East India Company was nearly bankrupt, with millions of pounds of unsold tea in its London warehouses.

The Tea Act was essentially a bailout of the East India Company. It actually reduced the price of tea, levying no new taxes, but keeping the three-penny tax on tea from before. Instead, the Tea Act gave the Company a one-shilling-per-pound subsidy on all tea sold in America. Now the Company could undersell the smugglers, and get rid of its surplus tea at a profit.

Bostonians would have none of it. In the first place, the Tea Act gave a monopoly to certain "**consignees**", who all turned out to be Governor Hutchinson's close friends and relatives. The town's merchants were outraged. If the royal officials could do this with tea, they could do it with other goods. No merchant or shopowner would be safe.

Furthermore, the Tea Act was seen as a ruse to get the colonists to pay the three-penny tax which they had so long opposed. The cry "No tax on tea!" echoed through the streets and in town meetings.

The Tea Act, then, managed to offend just about everyone in town, even many who had supported the Crown until now. The consignees were called "enemies of

the country"; America, one writer opined, was "threatened with worse than Egyptian slavery." Virtually no one, save the Governor and his consignees, wished the tea to be landed.

Or, as Abigail Adams put it, "The flame is kindled and like lightning it catches from soul to soul."

The Tea Party began, as we have seen, at Old South Meeting-House. From there, parti-

cipants and observers alike marched to Griffin's Wharf, where the three tea ships were docked. The ship's log of the *Dartmouth* provides this description:

"Between six and seven o'clock this evening came down to the wharf a body of about one thousand people. Among them were a number dressed and whooping like Indians. They came on board the ship, and, after warning myself and the Customs House officer to get out of the way, they unlaid the hatches and went down to the hold, where was 80 whole and 34 half chests of tea, which they hoisted upon deck, and cut the chests to pieces, and hove the tea off overboard, where it was damaged and lost."

The accursed tea, that worst of plagues, that pernicious and obnoxious herb, had been destroyed. While men and boys broke open the tea chests aboard the three ships, others waded in the harbor below, making sure that none of the leaves escaped the mud and muck. One man, caught stuffing his pockets with tea, had his coat ripped off and thrown in the harbor as well.

But care was taken that nothing save the tea was damaged. One padlock had to be forced open, but it was mysteriously replaced the next day.

"Depend upon it," wrote John Adams, "they were no ordinary Mohawks"; for the Tea Party was organized well in advance. Most of the 120 or so young men and boys had gathered secretly in taverns, houses, and warehouses while the crowds were meeting at Old South. Lamps and torches illuminated the nighttime scene "as light as day" as a thousand people watched from the shore.

Once the deed was done, all became quiet. There was no rejoicing that night; fear of British recrimination was too great. John Adams wrote that "The town of Boston was never more still and calm on a Saturday night."

What had been done boggles the mind even today. Destroyed were 342 chests, half-chests, and quarter-chests of tea, weighing 92,616 pounds in all — more than 46 tons of tea leaves, enough to brew 18,523,200 cups! The East India Company's losses mounted to £9,659, 6 shillings, and 4 pence; today the ruined tea would cost about a million dollars in the grocery store!

Stories spread around town of "the taste of their fish being altered", and some worried "that the fish may have contracted a disorder not unlike the nervous compaints of the human body" after being immersed in caffeinated harbor water.

Since no one was willing to talk, Parliament meted out punishment on the

entire town. The Boston Port Bill closed the harbor to all boats, even restricting ferries, until the townspeople paid for the tea. Boston, which had profited so much from the sea, found its economy now shut down completely.

To add insult to injury, another law abolished much of the colony's elected government. Other measures said that court trials could be moved to England, and that soldiers could be quartered in people's homes against their will.

These **"Intolerable Acts"** did not break the colonists' spirit, as Parliament had hoped. Instead, these strict measures ensured that people would resist even more strongly, with their lives if it came to that. And it soon did come to that.

The Boston Tea Party Ships & Museum

None of the original three ships survives today, but two, the *Beaver* and the *Eleanor*, have been re-created. They sit today in Fort Point Channel, where you can walk their decks, go below in the hold, and even heave a "chest of tea" into the water. The adjacent museum uses modern multimedia techniques to graphically tell the story of the radicals' moment of triumph. An authentic tea chest from 1773, one of two still extant, is the featured display.

Since visits are on a timed basis, you should allow at least an hour for your visit, more if you want to partake of the beverage in Abigail's Tea Room.

A mere tea chest's throw away from the museum complex is the site of old Griffin's Wharf, now occupied by an Intercontinental Hotel.

END OF SIDETRIP: If you visited the Tea Party Ships, walk back up Congress Street to the Old State House to resume your walk on the Freedom Trail.

From the Old State House, cross the intersection, then follow the Trail's red line half a block north on Congress Street, until you see Faneuil Hall on your right.

Faneuil Hall

"The Cradle of Liberty"

No local landmark is more cherished than this, the city's political focal point for over 2½ centuries. Boston's town meeting hall was where the colonists first dared to speak publicly against British rule. Here "was kindled that divine spark of liberty, which, like an unconquerable flame, has pervaded the continent."

The building was a gift to the town from **Peter Faneuil**, "the topmost merchant in all the town", in 1742. Faneuil's parents were *Huguenots*, or French Protestants, who came to British America fleeing religious persecution in their homeland. The unusual family name has always been a tongue-twister to non-French-speaking Yankees. Proper Bostonians still insist on

the "correct" pronunciation of *fannel* or even *funnel*, even though many locals now say *fanyel*. Alas, you'll often hear (horrors!) *fan-yoo-el* from the lips of newcomers and visitors.

Peter Faneuil inherited his fortune from his uncle Andrew, a prosperous merchant whose ships called at ports around the Atlantic. But legend says that Andrew's bequest was subject to one unusual provision: like his uncle, Peter had to remain a bachelor. If he ever married, he would forfeit the money!

Peter named one of his ships the *Jolly Bachelor*; and he must have been a jolly bachelor himself, for he died at age 43 of "too much good living", leaving behind a cellarful of wine, beer, and cheese.

In 1740 Peter Faneuil proposed, "at his Own proper Cost and Charge," to erect a **market** "to Encourage and accommodate the Countrey People who bring Provisions into this Town." This was a highly controversial issue in 18th-century Boston. When put to a vote, Faneuil's generous offer was accepted by a bare seven-vote margin, 367 for and 360 against.

So, to appease the opposition, Peter Faneuil added a **town meeting hall** on the second floor, above the market stalls. It has been so ever since: an exchange of goods below, and an exchange of ideas upstairs.

Faneuil Hall was gutted by fire in 1761. When it reopened in 1763, as tensions with mother England were starting to arise, James Otis prophetically dedicated the room to the "Cause of Liberty".

*As you approach Faneuil Hall from Congress Street, pause for a moment at Anne Whitney's **statue of Samuel Adams**, "a patriot" who "organized the Revolution".*

No other site could be more appropriate for a statue of Adams, the "Man of the Town-Meeting". Even Governor Hutchinson, his arch-enemy, admitted that Adams' "chief dependence is upon the Boston town-meeting." Here he "animated, enlightened, fortified, and roused the admiring throng; he seemed to gather them together... as a hen gathereth her chickens under her wings."

Yet unlike most politicians, Samuel Adams had no goals of personal gain. Indeed, he refused glory and fame whenever it was offered to him.

*The doors behind Adams' statue open into the ground-floor stores and the **National Park Visitor Center**, which houses an information desk, a bookstore, and restrooms. To visit the hall itself, walk around the building to its east end — facing Quincy Market's pillars — and enter through the center door. There are 21 steps up into the hall. Or you can go in the first floor, and take an elevator up.*

Faneuil Hall is frequently used for meetings and events. Most of these are public, but casual visitors aren't always admitted. When no meetings are underway, the hall is open, and National Park rangers give frequent presentations.

Here is the Cradle of Liberty where, in May 1764, Americans first protested the **Sugar Act** and set down the doctrine of "no taxation without representation". Or, as they put it then: "If taxes are laid upon us in any shape without our having a Legal Representation where they are laid, are we not reduced from the Character of Free Subjects to the miserable state of tributary Slaves?"

That was only the first of many momentous gatherings held here over the next decade. Bostonians came time and again to Faneuil Hall, mainly to protest but sometimes to rejoice. Here they rallied against the Stamp Act, the Townshend Acts, and the landing of British troops. Here was the funeral for the victims of the Boston Massacre. And here the people of Boston created a **Committee of Correspondence** to communicate news and opinion to other towns and colonies. "Let every town assemble," wrote Samuel Adams; but to the Tories, Adams' idea was "the source of the rebellion".

And here on November 5, 1773, led by John Hancock, Bostonians held the first of the **Tea Meetings** to discuss the fate of that "baneful weed".

After the Tea Party, British officials banned town meetings and restricted use of Faneuil Hall. The Cradle of Liberty became a barracks for troops, then a theatre for their amusement. One performance of a farce written by General Burgoyne was rudely interrupted by the news of an American attack. All of the actors and most of the audience rushed out to take their posts.

After the Revolution — and today

When he gave this hall to Boston in 1742, Peter Faneuil stipulated that it should always be open for public use; and in the centuries since, it has always been as he requested. In the mid-19th century, this hall was the chief rallying place of America's **anti-slavery movement**. Such famous abolitionists as Wendell Phillips, William Lloyd Garrison, and Frederick Douglass all spoke here.

Ironically, these rallies against slavery were held in a hall built with profits from the slave trade — for Peter Faneuil himself once dealt in human flesh.

Nor was all sentiment against slavery even in the 19th century. On one occasion, Faneuil Hall was the scene of a "truly eloquent" defense of slavery by Jefferson Davis, later to be the president of the Confederacy.

The **women's rights movement** also has deep roots here, and many early **temperance rallies** took place in Faneuil Hall. Nearly every American war from 1812 to Iraq has been debated within these walls.

Over the years, this sacred room has heard the voices of many famous — and not-so-famous — Americans. Faneuil Hall today is as busy as it ever has been. Just as in centuries past, radicals, rabble-rousers, and even insurance companies share the use of the hall with official city functions. It is the site of many a political oration; John F. Kennedy made the final campaign speech of his life here, the night before he was elected President in 1960. Also held here are orchestra concerts, naturalization ceremonies for new citizens, spelling bees, and once, even, an awards ceremony for Internal Revenue Service agents who had collected the most taxes!

More than a tourist attraction, this room is a living monument to free speech. Liberty, indeed, still "spreads its joyful wings over this place."

Or, as Wendell Phillips put it, "Those who cannot hear free speech had better go home. Faneuil Hall is no place for slavish hearts."

As you visit Faneuil Hall, keep in mind that the building was a great deal **smaller** in colonial days than it is now. Charles Bulfinch, the

FANEUIL HALL IN THE 1700s,
BEFORE ITS ENLARGEMENT

famous architect, enlarged it in 1806. Bulfinch kept the outer walls on three sides, but he doubled the area of the hall, raised the roof, and added the balcony. Some of the plaster decoration inside the hall dates back to the 1760s, but most of the interior is Bulfinch's.

The room is dominated by a life-size **portrait of Daniel Webster** speaking before the Senate in Washington, which hangs over the stage. This immense canvas, 16 feet high by 30 feet wide, was commissioned by King Louis-Philippe of France in 1842. But in the seven years it took artist G. P. A. Healy to complete the work, Louis-Philippe was deposed in a revolution. Instead of hanging at Versailles, the painting eventually came to Boston.

Upstairs over the hall is the **Armory Museum** of the **Ancient and Honorable Artillery Company**, which is open weekdays. The Ancients, as they are called, are America's first and oldest militia organization. Founded in 1637 to protect the colony against Indian attack, they were a "School for Officers and a Nursery for Soldiers". Members of the Company dumped tea into Boston Harbor and fought at Bunker Hill; indeed, they have fought in every American war since the 17th century. As a unit, however, their only service was with Myles Standish in a 1645 skirmish with

native Americans, and again in Shay's Rebellion in 1787.

Today they are largely a ceremonial organization, an inspiration to patriotism. Their armory, in Faneuil Hall's attic since 1746, contains relics from every period of Boston history. It is a fascinating place to explore.

If the wind is off the ocean, as it often is, the lane leading north, between the outdoor café and a low glass building, offers a fine view of Faneuil Hall's unusual **weathervane**.

The Grasshopper

No one knows why Peter Faneuil chose an insect to top off his market/meeting hall, but the grasshopper has been up there since 1742. There have been many theories over the years; but the best guess is that it was copied from the Royal Exchange in London, which had a similar weathervane, and of which Peter Faneuil was a member.

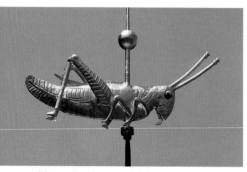

Shem Drowne, deacon and master craftsman, fashioned the weathervane out of copper and gold leaf, with glass doorknobs for its eyes. It is 52 inches long and weighs 38 pounds. A "vest" in the stomach contains coins and other mementos of its past.

Many years ago, a note was found, folded up, inside the vest. It read: "Shem Drowne made itt, May 25, 1742. To my brethren and fellow grasshoppers, Fell in ye year 1755, Novr 18th, early in ye Morning by a great Earthquake by my old Master above. Again Like to have Met with my Utter Ruin by Fire [in 1761], but hopping Timely from my Publick Scituation, Came of With Broken bones, & much Bruised. Cured and Again fixed, Old Master's Son, Thomas Drowne June 28th 1768, And Though I now promise to Discharge my Office, yet I shall very as ye Wind."

Besides the earthquake and fire, the insectiform weathervane also survived a grasshoppernapping in 1974. It was found less than a week later, wrapped in some old flags and hidden under the eaves of the cupola.

In 250 years, this unique landmark has become a symbol of Boston. During the War of 1812, legend has it, it was used to screen out spies, for "Anyone who claims to be a Bostonian and who does not know the shape of Faneuil Hall's weathervane must be an impostor."

Faneuil Hall Marketplace

The markets next to the Cradle of Liberty are today Boston's most popular gathering place. These three long buildings were built in 1826 as an extension of the market underneath Faneuil Hall itself. For nearly a century and a half, these markets fed Boston. But by the late 1960s, the food wholesalers had moved out, and these solid granite warehouses stood virtually empty.

Mayor Kevin White and architect Benjamin Thompson shared a brilliant idea: Restore the markets to their former grandeur, and convert them into an urban shopping mall. This "risky venture" succeeded beyond anyone's dreams. Today Faneuil Hall Marketplace is one of the busiest attractions in all America. Up to *eighteen million people* visit the markets every year!

Alexander Parris, the original architect, designed the markets as classic examples of the Greek Revival style. The central building, with its dome and portico, is officially "Faneuil Hall Market". But it's long been known as **"Quincy Market"**, after Josiah Quincy, who was Boston's mayor 180 years ago when it was built. The central corridor of this long building is still devoted entirely to food — now mostly fast-order takeout.

To either side, the **North Market** and **South Market** buildings were originally sold off like row houses to different market firms. Over the years, some were demolished or so altered that they had to be completely rebuilt when the markets were restored in 1976. Today they house a variety of shops and restaurants. Yet, in a sign of changing food habits, the North Market's famed **Durgin-Park Market Dining Rooms** closed early in 2019; their hearty Yankee cooking is now, alas! just a memory.

> *Inside the brick Faneuil Hall building, on the first floor, is a fascinating **re-creation of a colonial printing office**; be sure to check it out before you leave the markets.*
>
> *Just outside the hall, near the Sephora store, look for the larger-than-life **statue of Mayor Kevin White**, striding towards the markets, the creation of artist Pablo Eduardo. It's an appropriate place for a memorial to "the loner in love with his city": Mayor White counted the restoration of these markets as his proudest achievement.*

> *The next Freedom Trail site, the Paul Revere house, is ten minutes away in Boston's North End. Cross North Street behind Sephora, then follow the red line up **Union Street**. Boston's modern City Hall will be on your left, across a small park.*

Do not overlook the double **statue of Mayor James Michael Curley** which stands in this park. Boston's best-loved politician, Curley was mayor for four terms between 1914 and 1949. He was a friend of the poor, a Robin Hood who called Boston bankers the "State Street Wrecking Crew". "The Puritan has passed; the Anglo-Saxon is a joke; a new and better America is here," declared the Irish-blooded mayor.

Curley was renowned for his oratory, but he always had time to talk with the voters who returned him to office. This sculpture by Lloyd Lillie captures both sides of his personality. Feel free to sit down for a chat with His Honor.

> *In the park on your left, just beyond Mayor Curley's statue, are the glass towers of the Holocaust Memorial.*

New England Holocaust Memorial

Six glass towers reach for the sky, in remembrance of something that must never be forgotten. The Holocaust in Europe, from 1940 to 1945, was one of the most horrible acts ever perpetrated on a supposedly civilized planet: the systematic murder of millions of human beings, the attempted extermination of entire races and cultures.

Most of the victims were Jews, but Gypsies, Slavs, priests, intellectuals, union leaders, homosexuals, persons with disabilities, and others were also targeted for mass slaughter.

Designed by architect Stanley Saitowitz, the New England Holocaust Memorial was dedicated in 1995. The six towers recall the six death camps erected by the Nazis; etched into the glass walls are six million numbers, in memory of the six million Jews who were murdered.

The Holocaust Memorial's site here along the Freedom Trail reminds us that the struggle for freedom and human liberties is never-ending.

You are encouraged to walk the black granite path leading through the towers, and to reflect on the inscriptions. It is a Jewish tradition for visitors to leave a token, such as a stone, in memory of the deceased.

After visiting the Holocaust Memorial, cross back to the other side of Union Street and rejoin the Freedom Trail's red line.

The Blackstone Block

On the right side of Union Street is Boston's oldest commercial district, the Blackstone Block. The tiny alleys that punctuate this block are the last surviving remnants of the town's narrow 17th-century by-ways. Their names — Marsh Lane, Creek Square, Salt Lane, and Scott Alley — recall early landforms and property owners. Historical markers have been placed along these passageways, and you may want to explore them on your own.

Pause at the end of the block at the **Union Oyster House**. This brick house was built circa 1716. Three decades later, Hopestill Capen sold silks and fancy dress goods here "at the sign of the cornfields". Here too Isaiah Thomas published the

radical *Massachusetts Spy* before the Revolution. Louis-Philippe, future King of France, lived here in exile in the 1790s, and gave French lessons to the people of Boston.

The Oyster House, the oldest continuously operated restaurant in America, has been here since 1826. While the upstairs is expanded, the ground floor remains original. You can still sit at the half-round mahogany oyster bar where Daniel Webster was a regular patron. Be sure to look in through the front windows to see this bar, where Webster usually downed three dozen oysters and six tumblers of brandy at a single sitting.

*Bear right after the Oyster House onto narrow **Marshall Street**.*

In an era when many people could not read, taverns were often named for objects that could be pictured on a sign. Among Boston's watering spots of old were the Boston Stone, the Rose and Crown, the Bunch of Grapes, the Bell in Hand, and the Green Dragon. Some of these names have been restored to use today, as two modern taverns in the Marshall Street area have taken historic names.

The **Green Dragon**, named for the most famous of Boston's colonial taverns, is one of these. Years after Independence, Daniel Webster called the original Green Dragon Tavern the "Headquarters of the Revolution" for the many secret meetings that once transpired in its back rooms. The tavern also doubled as St. Andrew's Masonic lodge. It stood just around the corner from here at 84 Union Street; the building was torn down in 1828, and the site is now occupied by a parking garage.

On your right, just past today's Green Dragon, is a square brick house at an angle to the street. The **Ebenezer Hancock house**, built in 1767, was the home of John Hancock's brother. Ebenezer Hancock was the deputy-paymaster-general of the Continental Army; and his house once held 2½ million French crowns in gleaming silver coin, sent by Louis XVI to pay the American soldiers. It is now a law office.

Just beyond the Hancock house, look for the **Boston Stone**, set low into a wall near the door of a gift shop. This has been a local landmark since 1737. Thomas Child, a painter, brought it over from England before 1700 and used it as a millstone to grind pigments. After Child's death, the stone was forgotten until a landowner found it on his property. A neighbor dubbed it the Boston Stone, after the famous London Stone, and used it as a tavern advertisement. It has been here ever since.

Many people claim that the Stone once served as Boston's "zero milestone", but the facts show that this was never the case.

*Go past the Boston Stone, then turn right at the next corner onto **Hanover Street**.*

If you are lucky enough to be here on Friday or Saturday, you will see a true Boston institution, the **Haymarket**. Pushcart vendors have been selling produce here since Boston was founded. Today's Haymarket no longer sells hay, but it is a panoply of sights, sounds, and smells, a veritable orgy of fruits, vegetables, and even fish piled high on rickety wooden carts and tables. The variety is astounding, and the prices unbeatably low.

(continued on page 42)

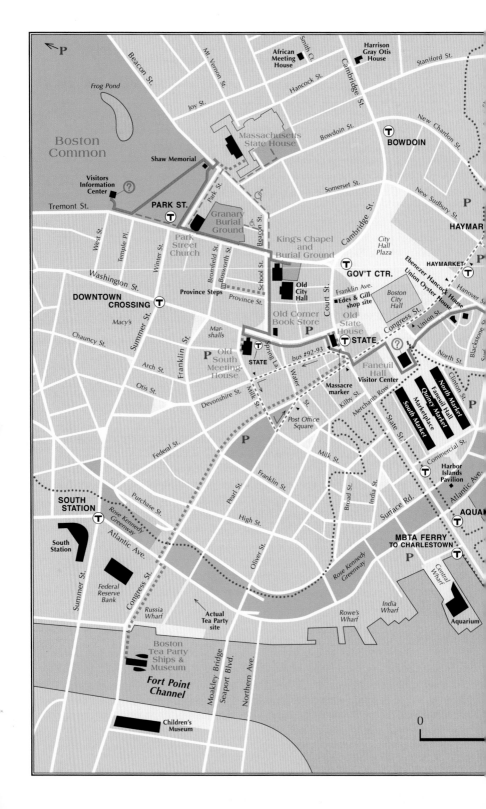

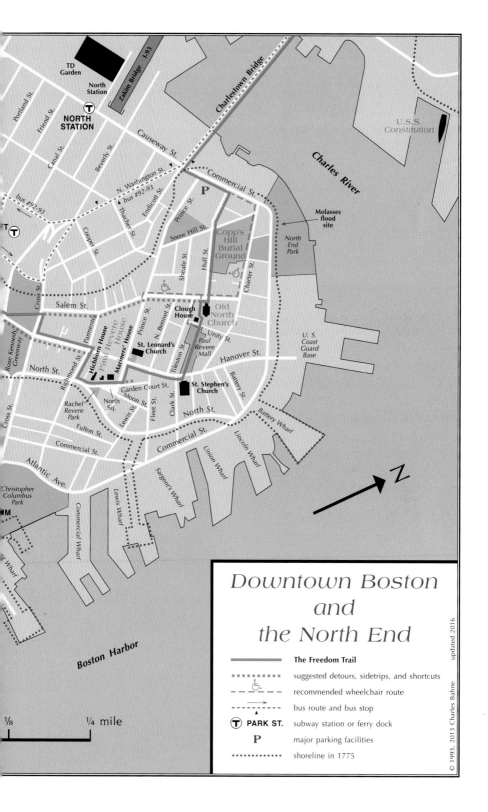

TD Garden

North Station

Zakim Bridge I-93

Charlestown Bridge

Charles River

U.S.S. Constitution

T NORTH STATION

Portland St.

Friend St.

Canal St.

Beverly St.

Causeway St.

N. Washington St. I-93

bus #92-93

T

bus #92-93

Cooper St.

Thacher St.

Endicott St.

Prince St.

Commercial St.

P

Molasses flood site

North End Park

Snow Hill St.

Copp's Hill Burial Ground

Sheafe St.

Hull St.

Charter St.

Cross St.

Salem St.

Parmenter St.

Prince St.

N. Bennet St.

Clough House

Old North Church

Rose Kennedy Greenway

Richmond St.

Paul Revere House

Hichborn House

St. Leonard's Church

Mariners' House

Unity St. Paul Revere Mall

Tileston St.

Hanover St.

U. S. Coast Guard Base

North St.

Garden Court St.

North Sq.

Moon St.

Fleet St.

Clark St.

St. Stephen's Church

Battery St.

Rachel Revere Park

Lewis St.

North St.

Battery Wharf

Fulton St.

Commercial St.

Commercial St.

Union Wharf

Lincoln Wharf

Cross St.

Atlantic Ave.

Sargent's Wharf

Christopher Columbus Park

M

Commercial Wharf

Lewis Wharf

g Wharf

N

Boston Harbor

⅛   ¼ mile

Downtown Boston and the North End

updated 2016

© 1993, 2013 Charles Bahne

━━━	**The Freedom Trail**
• • • • •	suggested detours, sidetrips, and shortcuts
♿ – – –	recommended wheelchair route
– – →	bus route and bus stop
T PARK ST.	subway station or ferry dock
P	major parking facilities
• • • • •	shoreline in 1775

The customers seem almost as assorted as the produce: businessmen, immigrants, college students, and little old Boston ladies with gigantic shopping bags, all vying for their vegetables. Every square millimeter of space, it seems, is packed either with food or with people.

Should the prices tempt you to buy, remember two rules: First, be watchful that you're not getting rotten produce or a heavy thumb on the scale. Second, never, *never* touch the display, lest you incur the lifelong wrath of a pushcart vendor.

In the adjacent buildings may be found equal bargains on meat, cheese, poultry, and eggs. This has been a street of butchers ever since 1666, when the town declared nearby Mill Creek — today's Rose Kennedy Greenway — as the only place in town for disposal of "garbidge, beast entrails, &c." Although their garbage dump is no longer outside their front door, the meat markets have stayed here for 3½ centuries!

*As you cross Blackstone Street, look carefully in the pavement for more modern "garbidge" cast in bronze. "**Asaroton**", a sculpture by Mags Harries, permanently recreates the clutter and litter of market day. The name means "unswept floor", and the concept dates from ancient Rome, where food was similarly portrayed on the mosaic tile floors in banquet halls.*

Beyond Blackstone Street, the parks of the **Rose Kennedy Greenway** mark the one-time site of Boston's elevated Central Artery expressway. In a decade-long construction project known as the "Big Dig", a new highway was built underground, and the overhead eyesore removed in 2004.

*The Freedom Trail jogs to the left, through the park. Directly ahead on the far side of the park is **Salem Street**, a street of butchers and grocers, and also a shortcut to the Old North Church. The Trail, however, leads first to Paul Revere's home. Follow the red line as it turns right, then left onto **Hanover Street**.*

The North End

Beyond the Greenway lies Boston's oldest and most colorful neighborhood. Once the home of Paul Revere and Thomas Hutchinson, the North End is now the city's Italian-American quarter. Shops and cafés line narrow, curving streets where Italian is as likely to be spoken as English.

In colonial days this was the "Island of North Boston", separated from the rest of town by Mill Creek. The creek, which powered tidal-operated flour mills, flowed where the Greenway is today. Two drawbridges spanned it, linking the North End with the mainland. Now, with the elevated highway gone, the North End is again reunited with the rest of the city.

Hanover Street is the North End's main street, lined with restaurants, cafés, bakeries, and stores. Calorie counters should be warned: the North End is a dieter's nightmare.

Boston's first neighborhood, the North End has been continually inhabited since the 1630s. Like the now-gone West and South Ends, this was chiefly a neighbor-

hood of tradesmen and mechanics. But amidst their modest houses were some of colonial Boston's finest mansions.

After independence, the North End quickly changed for the worse. Boston became a prosperous port, its waterfront a constant scene of activity. Busy, noisy, smelly wharves surrounded the district on three sides. **Sailors** who had not set foot on dry land in months, now suddenly given half a year's pay, roamed the streets in search of amusement. Decent people moved out of the North End to higher ground; by the mid-1800s, even *police officers* felt unsafe walking here alone!

Then came the **immigrants**. Irish families, fleeing famine in their homeland, crowded into the North End because they could not afford to live elsewhere. Within a decade, from 1845 to 1855, some 50,000 Irish immigrants settled in Boston. Their poverty, combined with the sailors' vices, turned this into the worst imaginable slum.

Eventually, of course, the Irish prospered and moved out, into the mainstream of Boston life. In their place, Jews from Eastern Europe and then Italians settled in the North End.

Today this is unquestionably an Italian neighborhood. By hard work over generations, Italian-Americans have built this former slum into a pleasant, respectable community where everyone seems to know everyone else — except, of course, for the tourists — and the streets are always lively.

*After walking a block on Hanover Street, turn right on **Richmond Street**. In the 1830s, this was the "Black Hole" or "Murder District", rife with bars, gambling dens, and lawless seamen. At the end of the block, **North Street** — then "Ann Street" — was notorious for its "nymphs" who entertained the sailors. After a police raid in 1851, the street was widened, the brothels razed, and even the street name changed to remove all traces of its indelicate past.*

North Street follows Boston's original shoreline; everything beyond it is filled land. Look down this street to the right, and you can see the golden cupola of Faneuil Hall, erected on the filled-in Town Dock of the 1600s.

*Turn left on North Street and keep on the left sidewalk, following the Freedom Trail into **North Square**.*

On your left, just beyond Baker's Alley and a pair of restaurants, is the **Pierce-Hichborn House**. This three-story brick house was built in 1711 for Moses Pierce, a glazier or glass merchant. Pierce's profession explains the house's many large windows, which were unusual for its day. In 1781 the house was purchased by Paul Revere's cousin, Nathaniel Hichborn. Hichborn, a shipwright, built boats at a wharf not far from here. The house is open for tours on most days; inquire at the Paul Revere House for details.

Just beyond the Hichborn house is the home of Paul Revere. You may want to walk across the street to get a better view. The entrance to both houses is through the brick-walled courtyard between them.

Paul Revere House

"Listen, my children, and you shall hear
Of the midnight ride of Paul Revere…" — *Longfellow*

This small wooden house in North Square is Boston's oldest structure, a last relic of the medieval town of the 1600s. Its fame, though, came nearly a hundred years after it was built. Late on the night of April 18, 1775, a middle-aged silversmith set out from this, his home, on a mission that would become legend.

Thanks to Longfellow's poem, Paul Revere is today America's most celebrated patriot, and his midnight ride the Revolution's best-known event. And thanks, too, to the poet's publicity, this house has been miraculously preserved for us to enjoy today.

Seventeenth-century North Square was a prosperous community of tradesmen and shopkeepers. Here, on the very site where Paul Revere would later live, was the childhood home of **Cotton Mather**, Puritan New England's most influential minister. Cotton's father, Increase Mather, was another noted minister, who preached at the Second Church in Boston just across the square.

But on a "Fatal & dismall day" in 1676, fire devastated North Square. Burnt were 45 houses including the Mather parsonage, the church, and several warehouses. Soon afterwards, the town imported its first fire engine.

The house you see today was built four years later, in 1680. Boston was just 50 years old; the Salem witch trials were yet 12 years away; and Paul Revere's grandfather was a young boy in France.

The house's first owner, Robert Howard, was a wealthy merchant who kept three or four slaves. This was a large and fashionable dwelling for its day. A central gable topped the roof, and its walls may have been covered with "roughcast" (a kind of stucco) for fireproofing. Similar houses adjoined to either side, making a row of three.

But by the time Paul Revere bought this house in 1770, it was 90 years old and no longer fashionable. It was also larger. An early modernization had added a partial third floor — which was removed early in the 20th century to "restore" the house to its "original" 1680 appearance.

With the now-gone third story, the house had seven rooms, plus a basement. It was quite a comfortable home for the Revere family in 1770: Paul, his wife Sara, their five children, and Paul's mother Deborah.

In all, Revere fathered sixteen children over a 29-year period. Five of them died young, and at most eight children ever lived at home at any one time. Paul's first wife, Sara, died at age 37 from complications of childbirth of her eighth baby. Revere remarried within six months, and his second wife Rachel bore him eight more children.

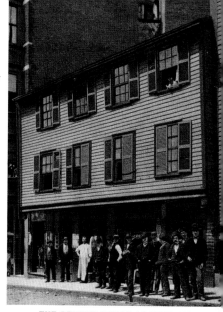

THE REVERE HOUSE AROUND 1900, BEFORE ITS RESTORATION

Revere's career

As a "mechanic" or craftsman, Paul Revere fit well into the North Square community. Brothers, sisters, and cousins lived nearby, and his shop was just two blocks away. Other neighbors included a "respectable soap-boiler" whose son was the president of Harvard College, plus several "joiners" or carpenters, two tailors, and another silversmith.

Silversmithing was a handsome trade to have in colonial America. Since there were no banks, families were obliged to keep their money at home. Silver coins were easily melted down into useful or decorative objects such as teapots and trays. Today Paul Revere silver is prized as some of the finest American work of that era.

Yet times were often hard. To make ends meet, Revere branched out into other fields. He made false teeth and sold dentifrice. For a small fee, he would make a copperplate engraving of any subject, from business cards to cartoons. His celebrated engravings of political subjects were popular, even if they were short on artistic merit.

After the Revolution, Revere became an early industrialist. He discovered methods of rolling sheet copper, and he cast some of the first bells ever made in America. The company he started, Revere Copper and Brass, pioneered the manufacture of copper-bottomed cookware in 1939.

Revere as a patriot

It is for his politics that Paul Revere is best known today. Revere's closest friend, Joseph Warren, guided him into Boston's political clubs long before anyone even thought of revolution. The North Caucus, the Masons, the Sons of Liberty — Revere was a member of them all. Most important, he was one of the trusted few who met in the **"long room"** over Edes and Gill's printing office on Queen Street.

In a room full of merchants and lawyers, all college-educated, Revere may have seemed out of place. But if this craftsman could not make speeches or write political tracts, Paul Revere still knew how to arouse popular feelings. His engravings were effective propaganda both at home and abroad. And he was a master at organizing spectacles, such as the 1765 celebration of the Stamp Act repeal held on Boston Common.

Another of his spectacles was the "very Striking Exhibition at the Dwelling House of Mr. Paul Revere, fronting old North Square," on the first anniversary of the Boston Massacre. All Boston, it seemed, flocked here that evening in 1771 to view the performance. Pictures in the upper windows, illuminated by candlelight, graphically depicted the events of a year before. "The whole was so well executed that the Spectators, which amounted to many Thousands, were struck with Solem Silence & their Contenances covered with a meloncholy Gloom."

Besides organizing the masses, Revere was also a trusted **express rider** who carried messages to distant colonies. His first documented ride was for the Committee of Correspondence in 1773. Revere was one of six riders who warned other seaports not to allow the tea ships to land their cargo.

A few weeks later, Revere carried news of the Tea Party south to New York and Philadelphia, departing without any sleep after he had spent the night dumping tea into the harbor. Altogether, Paul Revere tallied thousands of miles as a courier for the patriot cause.

Revere's most famous ride took him just thirteen miles to Lexington; but it would be nearly a year before he dared set foot in his hometown again. Rachel and the children joined him in nearby Watertown, and his oldest son Paul stayed here in Boston to protect his house and his workshop from plunder by British troops.

The Revere house today

Revere sold this house in 1800, and it suffered with the neighborhood. Over the decades it was a boarding house, a tenement, a cigar factory, and a bank. Miraculously, though, it survived nearly intact. In 1905 a group of Revere's descendants purchased the house and began its restoration.

As we have seen, the restoration included removal of the 18th-century additions, so that today the outside bears little resemblance to the three-story house that Paul Revere knew. But inside, about 90 percent of the structure is original. Even

some of Revere's wallpaper survives and can be seen. The period furnishings include a few pieces from the family.

Visitors may enter through the courtyard into the kitchen and the hall (what we'd call a "living room" now). Upstairs are two chambers ("bedrooms" today), and in the courtyard, a 900-pound bell cast by Revere is on display.

*Follow the red line past the Revere house and through triangular **North Square**. In Revere's day, this was the site of a town pump, and of weekly market days.*

North Square

A century before Revere, North Square was the home of a **Captain Kemble**. When the captain returned home in 1673 from a three-year-long ocean voyage, he lovingly kissed his wife on their doorstep. Unfortunately for him, though, it was a Sunday. For defiling the Sabbath with his "lewd and unseemly conduct", Captain Kemble had to stand two hours in the town stocks!

In another era, the "lewd and unseemly conduct" of thousands of sailors — and of the nearby "nymphs" — prompted the organization of many religious missions to the seamen. One of those, the **Mariners' House**, still stands just two doors beyond the Paul Revere House. Since 1847 the red brick building with the anchor on its front has been a haven to sailors in a strange port, offering them food, lodging, and counsel — a little bit of God's work in a quarter that was once generally abandoned to the devil.

Across the square is the **bethel**, or church, where Father Edward Taylor once preached to Boston's seamen. Like many other orphans, Taylor went to sea when he was just seven years old. Ten years later, on a port visit to Boston, Taylor passed by a church on a hot Sunday morning and heard the sermon through an open window. He soon became a minister himself, spreading the word of God to other seafaring men. When Charles Dickens visited Boston, he came to hear the "sailor preacher", and the great English author sat in a side pew next to a lame, one-eyed mariner.

Father Taylor's bethel is now an Italian Catholic church; a small plaque on its front shows its original appearance. But the Mariners' House remains today, offering lodging to seamen — seamen only! — for a bargain price.

SIDETRIP: Instead of turning left at the next corner, leave the red line for a brief moment and walk straight ahead for a few yards, onto Garden Court Street.

Garden Court Street

This narrow lane leading out of North Square was once the site of two of colonial Boston's grandest dwellings. At the corner, where a souvenir store is now, lived wealthy merchant **William Clark**, after whom North Square was once called "Clark's Square". Clark's 26-room mansion was later bought by Sir Harry Frankland, the royal collector of customs. Eccentric Sir Harry often rode his pony up the broad stairs of his three-story home.

Next door to Frankland lived **Thomas Hutchinson**, last civilian governor of the Massachusetts colony. "Tommy Skin-and-Bones", as the patriots called him, was "the principal object of popular resentment" before the Revolution. No other Tory was so prominent, or so powerful, as he.

A native Bostonian, Thomas Hutchinson loved Massachusetts. Yet he never understood it. A devout Loyalist, he proudly boasted, "I now represent the greatest monarch on earth." His loyalty was rewarded, of course, with frequent appointments to royal offices. But to many citizens, Hutchinson was an opportunist who supported the Crown only to further his own career.

Sometimes people's resentment turned to violence. On the night of August 26, 1765, during the protests against the Stamp Act, a mob descended on Lt. Gov. Hutchinson's home just as he and his family were sitting down to supper.

As he put it later, "The hellish crew fell upon my house with the rage of devils." His money and his silver were stolen, his wine drunk, his furniture smashed to kindling, all because of his supposed support for the hated tax. "They began to take the slate and boards from the roof, and were prevented only by the approaching daylight from a total demolition of the building." By dawn, he wrote, "One of the best finished houses in the province had nothing remaining but the bare walls and floors…. Such ruin was never seen in America."

After the Tea Party, Thomas Hutchinson was recalled to England to meet with George III. The war broke out before he could return. He died, it is said, of a broken heart, longing for the homeland which he could never see again.

Both Hutchinson's house and the Clark-Frankland mansion next door disappeared long ago, torn down to make way for an 1834 street-widening project. Today the only reminder of their elegance is a bronze plaque mounted on the left side wall where Hutchinson's house once stood.

In the 19th century this little street produced another famous resident. **Rose Fitzgerald (Kennedy)** was born in 1890 in a now-demolished house at 4 Garden Court Street, just across from the Hutchinson house site. The granddaughter of Irish immigrants, Rose became the mother of President John F. Kennedy. Her father, John F. Fitzgerald, was a custom-house clerk whose activity in ward politics soon made him a congressman and then mayor of Boston. But Rose did not grow up here in the North End; as his political career blossomed, "Honey Fitz" quickly moved his family into the more prestigious suburbs, where his daughter spent her formative years.

END OF SIDETRIP: Walk back to North Square; turn at the corner and follow the red line along Prince Street. At the next intersection, turn right onto Hanover Street.

Across Hanover Street is **St. Leonard's Church** with its well-tended Peace Garden. Completed in 1899, this was Boston's first church building erected by an Italian congregation. The sanctuary boasts ornate religious artwork crafted by the immigrant artisans who built it.

In the summer, you may find yourself in the middle of a *festa*, or **Italian street festival**. Nearly every weekend in July and August sees a celebration somewhere in the North End, each one honoring a different patron saint. Many of these "feasts" take place along or near Hanover Street. Feel free to join in the festivities, or come back at night, when the fun really begins.

At the bend in Hanover Street is a red brick church topped by a white cupola and a gold dome. **St. Stephen's Church** is the only survivor of the five Boston church buildings designed by architect Charles Bulfinch. Originally known as "New North Church", it was erected in 1804 to house a Unitarian congregation. In 1862 the building was sold to a Roman Catholic parish for $35,000. Rose Fitzgerald was baptized here in 1890.

Visitors are welcome in St. Stephen's, which is restored to its early 19th-century appearance. Inside the vestibule, exhibits show some of the church's history, including pieces of the Paul Revere copper which originally covered the cupola dome. Revere's firm also made the church's first bell.

*Cross Hanover Street to the **Paul Revere Mall**, a one-half-acre park honoring the famous patriot. In one of the city's most-photographed scenes, a statue of Revere gallops through the Mall while, in the distance, the tower of Old North Church looms over the Midnight Rider's shoulder.*

The Midnight Ride of Paul Revere

Like any famous event, the Midnight Ride of Paul Revere has given birth to many legends and myths over the years. Revere's "publicity agent", Henry Wadsworth Longfellow, was a poet and not a historian, and therein lies much of the confusion. Let us pause a moment to set the record straight.

The best description of the "Eighteenth of April, in Seventy-five" comes from Revere's own words, which we shall quote in the next few pages. (The spellings are Revere's, too.)

By 1775, Paul Revere was the patriots' most trusted messenger, having already carried their secrets for thousands of miles. That winter, he also became "one of upwards of thirty, cheifly mechanics, who formed our selves in to a Committee for the purpose of watching the Movements of the British Soldiers, and gaining every intelegence of the movements of the Tories."

Three days before the Midnight Ride, this committee observed that "the Boats belonging to the Transports were all launched," and

"that the Grenadiers & light Infantry were all taken off duty. From these movements, we expected something serious was [to] be transacted."

So on Sunday, April 16, two days before his more famous ride, Paul Revere made his first ride to Lexington to warn that something was afoot.

On his way back home that Sunday, Revere "returned at Night thro Charlestown; there I agreed with a Col. Conant, & some other Gentlemen, that if the British went out by Water, we would Shew two Lanthorns in the North Church Steeple; & if by Land, one, as a Signal; for we were aprehensive it would be dificult to Cross the Charles River, or git over Boston neck."

The lanterns were thus not signals to Revere "on the opposite shore" — as Longfellow put it — but signals *from* Revere, in case he was unable to escape safely with the news from British-occupied Boston.

"On Tuesday evening, the 18th," Revere writes, "it was observed, that a number of Soldiers were marching towards the bottom of the Common. About 10 o'Clock, Dr. Warren Sent in great haste for me, and beged that I would imediately Set off for Lexington, where Messrs. Hancock & Adams were, & aquaint them of the Movement, and that it was thought they [Hancock and Adams] were the objets."

The patriots were unsure about the British troops' mission that night. The common belief was that the redcoats would try to arrest John Hancock and Samuel Adams, staying at the Clarke parsonage in Lexington. In fact, however, the soldiers marched to seize munitions stored at Concord, seven miles beyond Lexington.

"When I got to Dr. Warren's house, I found he had sent an express by land to Lexington — a Mr. Wm. Daws." While Revere went one way, William Dawes was already enroute via a different road. This was merely insurance against one rider or the other being captured.

To get out of Boston, Revere had to row across the Charles River, passing under the guns of the British Navy ship *Somerset*, anchored in mid-river just to prevent anyone from crossing. Dawes, who went by land, had to pass through a British Army checkpoint at Boston Neck, and convince the guards there of his innocence.

Then both men had to ride through a countryside teeming with patrols, who were on the lookout for messengers such as they. A third rider, sent from Charlestown, never made it to Lexington.

Revere goes on: "I left Dr. Warrens, called upon a friend, and desired him to make the Signals. I then went Home, took my Boots & Surtout [overcoat], & went to the North part of the Town, Where I had kept a Boat; two friends rowed me across Charles River, a little to the eastward where the Somerset Man of War lay. It was then young flood [tide], the Ship was winding, & the moon was Rising."

If it had been just fifteen minutes later, some historians suggest, the rising moon would have been so bright that Revere would surely have been caught.

The story is told that when Revere and his two friends got to his rowboat, they lacked cloth to muffle the sound of the oars. Afraid to go back to their own houses, one friend went to his sweetheart's. After a whispered conversation, the window was thrown open, and the "fair daughter of liberty" tossed down a flannel petticoat supposedly "still warm from the wearer's body."

In Charlestown, Revere "got a Horse of Deacon Larkin" and set off; "it was then about 11 o'Clock, & very pleasant." He started to take the most direct route, but it was blocked by "two Officers on Horse-back, standing under the shade of a Tree." One of these British soldiers chased Revere for "about 300 Yardes" until the redcoat's horse got mired in mud.

Revere then took a longer road through Medford, where "I awaked the Captain of the Minute men; & after that, I alarmed almost every House, till I got to Lexington."

He arrived just after midnight. The parsonage where Hancock and Adams were staying was guarded by minute men, who would not let Revere in. The ladies and gentlemen were sleeping, the sergeant said, and had "requested that they might not be disturbed by any noise about the house."

"Noise!" replied Revere. "You'll have noise enough before long! The Regulars are coming out!!"

Hancock, hearing the familiar voice, called, "Come in, Revere, we are not afraid of *you*."

William Dawes, who had left Boston an hour earlier but who followed a longer route, arrived half an hour after Revere.

Their official mission — to warn Hancock and Adams — was now completed; but after rest and refreshment the two couriers decided to set out for Concord.

Along the way, they met Dr. Samuel Prescott, a "high Son of Liberty" who was returning home from courting his fiancée. (It was now well after 1:00 AM.) Prescott joined the other two riders on their errand of alarm.

Halfway to Concord, however, the party was stopped by another British patrol. Prescott escaped and got the news through to Concord. Dawes fled, too, by bluffing the redcoat soldiers, but he fell off his horse and never got to Concord. Paul Revere was arrested. One officer "Clap'd his Pistol to my head, and said he was going to ask me some questions, if I did not tell the truth, he would blow my brains out.... We rode [back towards Boston] till we got near Lexington Meeting-house, when the

Militia fired a Voley of Guns, which appeared to alarm them very much."

Surprised by the minute men's practice volley, the British major released Revere. But Paul had to walk, for the horse, the "very good Horse" of Deacon Larkin, was kept by the redcoats, the first prisoner of this now-imminent war.

Revere went back to Adams and Hancock "and told them what had happined." All three now fled to Woburn, a few miles distant.

Revere returned to Lexington one more time that morning, to retrieve a trunk of Hancock's secret papers. Dawn was now breaking.

"While we were giting the Trunk," Revere wrote, "we saw the British very near, upon a full March…. [I] had not got half Gun shot [about 100 yards] off, When the Minesteral Troops appeared in sight, behinde the Meeting House; they made a short halt. When one gun was fired, I heard the report, turned my head, and saw the smoake in front of the Troops, they imeaditly gave a great shout, ran afew paces, and then the whole fired."

The War had begun.

Revere got not a penny for this, his most famous ride, although he was paid for some of his longer journeys. Nor did he seek fame for what he had done. During his own lifetime Paul Revere was better known for his work as a silversmith and as a manufacturer than as a midnight rider.

It was not for 85 years that Paul Revere's ride became a household word. One day in April 1860, Henry Wadsworth Longfellow visited the Old North Church with his friend George Sumner and a "Mr. Harris of North End, who acts as our guide…." The next day Longfellow began drafting his poem. Published that December, it turned Paul Revere into a national hero virtually overnight.

Go through the Mall, towards the steeple where Revere's signal lanterns were hung.

The Paul Revere Mall — also known locally as "the Prado" — was created by the city during the Great Depression. But the **statue of Revere** carrying the news "through every Middlesex village and farm" was sculpted over 50 years earlier. Artist Cyrus Dallin, who first conceived the work as a young man, was nearly 80 when it finally found a home.

On the south (left) wall of the park are 13 **bronze panels**, by sculptor Robert Savage Chase, showing the history of the North End and its people.

As you cross narrow Unity Street, notice the three-story brick house just to your left.

Erected about 1715, this home was the work of brick mason **Ebenezer Clough**, who constructed a row of houses here. A few years later, Clough also built the nearby Old North Church. The only survivor of the row, this historic dwelling had a third story added in 1808. Now owned by the church, it features fascinating exhibits including a colonial chocolate shop.

To the right of the Clough House, where the courtyard is today, stood an identical house, also the work of Clough, and once owned by Benjamin Franklin. Ben's sister, Jane Mecom, lived here, and Ben himself stayed here when he visited his family. That house was taken down in the 1930s.

Walk across Unity Street, through the courtyard, and up the steps to the Old North Church. (If the gate is locked, or if you cannot climb stairs, then turn left past the Clough House, right at the corner onto Tileston Street, and right again on Salem Street to the church.)

Old North Church

"One, if by land, and two, if by sea"

The steeple of Old North Church, towering heavenward over the North End, is perhaps Boston's most famous landmark. Here, on the night of April 18, 1775, the signal lanterns of Paul Revere shone to warn the country of the British troops' march. Few events in our nation's history are so well known as this daring act of military intelligence on the eve of our Revolution.

As we have seen, Revere "called upon a friend, and desired him to make the Signals." That friend was young **Robert Newman**, the church sexton.

Newman faced one major problem: His mother's house, just a block away from the church, was full of British Army officers who were quartered there. To avoid their suspicion, Newman pretended to go to sleep early; then he climbed out of his upstairs bedroom window to meet Revere at a prearranged rendezvous somewhere on the streets of the North End.

The instructions given, Newman entered the church and started up the tower steps. Another friend, John Pulling, locked the door behind Newman and waited, standing guard, below.

The **"glimmer, and then a gleam of light"** must have shone for only a moment or two. The people in Charlestown were alert for the signals. But if anyone else saw the flickering candle flame, there could be trouble indeed. Soldiers were everywhere in the streets, and even an innocent passerby might "see the light and scream 'fire'."

His deed done, Newman left through a church window, not daring to unlock the door again. Back at home, he clambered over a roof and into his bedroom window. Yet for all of his precautions, Robert Newman was arrested and questioned a few days later. He successfully convinced the British authorities of his innocence, and then he fled town.

The Old North is also **Boston's oldest standing church building**. It opened for worship on December 29, 1723, and is still used today by the same congregation. Bookseller William Price adapted the design from books showing Sir Christopher Wren's many London churches. Ebenezer Clough and his partner built the walls, 2½ feet thick, out of 513,654 bricks that were made in nearby Medford.

Officially, this has always been **"Christ Church in Boston"**. "Old North" is just a nickname, given historically to the North End's oldest church building. Over the years, there have been several different "Old Norths" in Boston, including a wooden

church in North Square that was standing across from Paul Revere's house in 1775. This has been a source of much confusion. Suffice it to say that Christ Church is, indeed, the one where Paul Revere's lanterns really did hang. The other "Old North" didn't even have a steeple tall enough to be seen in Charlestown.

At 191 feet, Christ Church's **steeple** has always been Boston's tallest. Twice it has been blown over by hurricanes, first in 1804 and again in 1954. The present steeple faithfully copies the original design, from which, on September 13, 1757, "John Childs who had given public notice of his intention to fly from the steeple… performed to the satisfaction of a great number of spectators." Childs made three flights, once firing a pistol in midair. Alas, no one recorded exactly *how* he flew.

Inside the brick tower are the first set of **bells** ever brought to English America. Cast in Gloucester, England, in 1744, this "peal" of eight bells was installed later that same year. The first bellringers were seven neighborhood boys — among them 15-year-old Paul Revere — who in 1750 signed a contract "once a week on Evenings To Ring the Bells for two hours Each time… and that We will Attend To Ring at any Time when the Wardens of the Church Aforesaid shall desire it." In later years, the bells were rung to celebrate the repeal of the Stamp Act, and the news of Cornwallis' final surrender at Yorktown.

Inside, "Old North" is virtually unchanged from the colonial era. High box pews ward off drafts, and brass chandeliers, given by Capt. William Maxwell and first used on Christmas eve of 1724, still illuminate the evening services. Also worthy of note are the church's first clock and the case of the first organ built in America, both still in use after more than two centuries. (The organ's works, however, have been replaced several times over the years.) Except for three years during the Revolution, Christ Church has been open for worship each Sunday since it was built.

To the right of the altar is the **window** through which Robert Newman fled in 1775. Bricked over for decades, it was discovered and reopened in 1989. On the left of the pulpit is a

bust of George Washington, placed in the church in 1815, the first public memorial erected to him in America. General Lafayette, a close friend of Washington's, called it "more like him than any other portrait."

Like King's Chapel, this was an Anglican, or Church of England, congregation. But the parishioners of Christ Church's were merchants, not government officials. The taxes imposed by Parliament had hurt many of them; so, compared to other New England Anglicans, they were far more liberal and tolerant of rabble-rousers who were preaching opposition to the mother country's policies.

Among the parishioners was Paul Revere's son, Joseph Warren Revere, whose name may still be seen above pew 54.

Under the church are 37 **crypts** containing the graves of some 1,100 people. Among these is Major John Pitcairn, leader of the first British companies to reach Lexington and Concord, who died at the Battle of Bunker Hill. Pitcairn's body was to have been sent back to Westminster Abbey, but it seems that the wrong corpse was sent to England by mistake. So Pitcairn is still here, while in London a Lieutenant Shea takes his place.

If you have time, be sure to inquire about the special "Behind the Scenes" and "Bones & Burials" tours, which are available for an additional fee, and which include the crypts and other areas that are normally not accessible.

Next to the church, a **gift shop** occupies the former Italian Episcopal Chapel building, erected in 1918.

Old North is one of the Freedom Trail buildings that you should definitely go into, even if your tour has been somewhat rushed. But remember, this is a church, to be treated with respect.

When he laid the cornerstone in 1723, Rev. Samuel Myles exclaimed, "May the gates of Hell never prevail against it!" And so far they haven't.

*Leaving the church, follow the Freedom Trail line up Hull Street. As you ascend the hill, be sure to pause about two-thirds of the way up and look back for a fine **view** of the church.*

*(If you can't climb stairs, you'll get a better view of Copp's Hill Burial Ground from **Charter Street**, a block to the right, than from Hull Street — but the graveyard's Charter Street gate is kept locked. Charter Street's hill is also much less steep. To rejoin the Trail and go to Charlestown, follow Charter Street to its end, then turn left on Commercial Street.)*

Throughout the North End, you'll see signs of "progress" as walk-up flats are being converted into luxury condominiums. Sadly, the North End has been "discovered" by outsiders. Families who have lived here for generations can no longer afford the rents; corner stores and meat markets have given way to tourist-oriented shops; and fewer and fewer residents are Italian. Even the street festivals have lost much of the old-country atmosphere they had just a few years ago. It's said that the North End as we know it is dying — so enjoy it while you can.

At the top of the hill on Hull Street, turn right over the high granite steps and through the gate into the burying ground.

Copp's Hill Burying Ground
The North End's neighborhood burying place

This summit, sometimes facetiously called "Corpse Hill", is the North End's oldest landmark. Its name comes from William Copp, a 17th-century shoemaker who owned the land before the town bought it for burials. Little is known about Copp, except that two of his grandchildren are buried here, their gravestone still visible near the crest of the hill.

Copp's Hill has always been the North End's highest piece of land. At first the Puritans set up their windmills here and called it Windmill Hill. It became a burial ground in 1660.

During the Revolution, British soldiers camped among the gravestones; and in the Battle of Bunker Hill, they fired shells on Charlestown from this summit.

Unlike King's Chapel and the Granary, Copp's Hill contains the graves of few famous people. Most of those buried here were ordinary North Enders, some wealthy, some not. Thus this is a fine place for epitaph reading, and for learning about the unsung heroes of ages past.

Some interesting inscriptions can be found in the area to the right of the main path. Here you'll find **Thomas Williston**, "who exchanged this Life for a better" in 1775, aged 75 years. "Stop here my friend & cast an Eye, As you are now, so once was I, As I am now, so you must be, Prepare for Death, and follow Me." Or **Francis Smith**, dead at age 20 in 1798: "Death with his Dart has Pierced my heart, When i was in my Prime."

Follow the path away from the gate until you come to a cross path. Here, at the peak of the hill, is the best view. Directly ahead is the Charlestown Navy Yard, on the far side of the Charles River. To your left, through the trees, you may get a glimpse of the Bunker Hill Monument.

Near the Charter Street gate at the bottom of the hill is the tomb of the **Mather** family. Here are buried two of 17th-century Boston's most learned — and most powerful — men. Increase and Cotton Mather, father and son, were both ministers, both active in politics. Their family was a literal dynasty which charted the

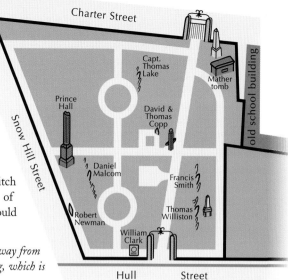

course of Puritanism in Massachusetts.

The younger Mather is best known today for his 1689 book *Memorable Providences, Relating to Witchcrafts and Possessions*, which helped fuel the witch hysteria in nearby Salem. After the witch trials began, however, both of the Mathers did all they could to stop them.

Follow the cross path away from the large school building, which is now condominiums.

You may wish to look for the grave of **Capt Thomas Lake**, who was "perfidiously slain by yᵉ Indians" in 1676. To find it, turn right at the first path and follow the circle two-thirds of the way around to the right. Now look a few gravestones in from the path. A hole in the top of the stone once contained metal from the bullets removed from the captain's body.

Otherwise, continue on the main crosspath to the tall black column in honor of **Prince Hall**, a leader of Boston's early free black community. Like many other free blacks in the late 1700s, he settled at the foot of Copp's Hill in a section called "New Guinea". Over a thousand African-American men, women, and children are buried on this side of the graveyard.

A leather dresser and a former slave, Prince Hall fought both British tyranny and racist attitudes at home. He served in the Continental Army, opposed slavery, and helped sponsor Boston's first school for black children. But he is best known as the father of African-American freemasonry, the founder of **African Lodge No. 1**, chartered in 1784. This was the first Masonic lodge in America with a charter from England, and the first black Masonic lodge in the world.

To the left along the Snow Hill Street fence, tomb number 27 contains the mortal remains of **Robert Newman**, the church sexton who hung Paul Revere's

"lanthorns" in the Old North Church.

But Copp's Hill's most interesting grave is behind you. From Prince Hall's granite column, walk back towards the top of the hill. Next to the interpretive marker, look for the row of gravestones with James B. Smith at the end; then turn right and go to the tallest stone in the vicinity.

This is the grave of "**Capt. Daniel Malcom,** Merchᵗ." Malcom, a member of the Sons of Liberty, was remembered for smuggling 60 casks of wine into port without paying the duty. When he died, he asked to be buried "in a Stone Grave 10 feet deep", safe from British bullets. All this is duly noted on his headstone.

But while Malcom's body may have been safe from British bullets, his gravestone was not! You can still see the scars made by redcoat soldiers who singled out this patriot's gravemarker for their target practice.

Alas, the British Army weren't the last to practice vandalism at Copp's Hill. Even after the burial ground was cleaned up in the 1840s, its neighbors did not always appreciate its history. A 19th-century superintendent found dozens of gravestones being used on roofs, in cellars, and once, even, as the oven floor in a bakery! This last use was a dead giveaway (pardon the pun), for the loaves of bread sold by the bakery had epitaphs burned into the bottom crust!

Now return to the entrance gate.

Before you leave, look for the tomb of **William Clark**, along the fence about 20 feet to the right of the gate. This is the same William Clark, "Eminent Merchant", who once lived in North Square. His epitaph describes him as "A Despiser of Sorry Persons and Little Actions." But what the tombstone does not say is that the "Mortal Part of William Clark" is no longer underneath it. Clark's body was removed, not long after he died, by Samuel Winslow, who took the tomb for himself and had his own name carved on the stone. A Sorry Person and a Little Action, indeed.

*As you leave the burial ground, be sure to notice the small wooden house across the street. Only 10½ feet wide at the front — and just 6' 2" deep in some interior rooms — it is assuredly the **narrowest house in Boston**. It's a private residence, so please don't disturb the occupants.*

⊷ ❊ ⊶

From Copp's Hill you may either call it a day and head back to Faneuil Hall; or you may continue across the river, following the Freedom Trail into Charlestown.

☞ **To return to Faneuil Hall and downtown,** *walk back down the hill to Old North Church. At Salem Street, in front of the church, turn right. Unlike the Freedom Trail, this route is not marked, but it's easy to follow. Just keep walking straight on Salem Street until you come to the Rose Kennedy Greenway, near where you entered the North End.*

☞ **If you want to go to the subway,** *follow the above directions; the Haymarket T station is just on the other side of the Greenway, to your right.*

If you have an appetite, don't overlook the small bakeries which offer delicious squares of pizza for a ridiculously low price. Or you may want to consider dinner in one of the North End's many restaurants. For dessert or a snack, try a pastry shop or an Italian caffè *on Hanover Street.*

☞ **To continue on the Freedom Trail to Charlestown,** *turn right on Hull Street as you leave the burial ground. Follow the red line down the other side of the hill, away from Old North.*

As you walk down the hill, notice the old **parking garage** on your left. Believe it or not, this is also a historic site. During the early morning of January 17, 1950, nine men broke into this garage, part of which was rented to the Brink's Armored Car Company. The famed **Brink's robbery** netted over $1,219,000 in cash, only a tiny fraction of which was ever recovered.

When you reach Commercial Street at the bottom of the hill, pause for a moment to see if you can detect the sweet aroma of molasses. Near here was the site of Boston's famous **molasses flood.** Across the street, to the right of where the ice skating rink is now, once stood a 2,300,000-gallon tank of molasses used to make munitions during World War I.

On January 15, 1919, the tank burst. A 25-foot-high wave of sticky goo flooded the area, knocking down everything in its wake. One policeman "beat it out in the race, for I rushed up a side street." He was lucky; 20 people and innumerable horses drowned in the stuff. Curious sightseers tracked molasses all over the city, leaving a tacky residue on virtually every pay phone and trolley seat. Decades later, old-timers claimed that you could still smell molasses around here on hot summer days.

How slow *is* molasses in January? Faster than you think — faster than some unfortunate souls could run!

At the foot of the hill turn left onto Commercial Street. Then at the first light, turn right and cross the Charlestown Bridge, keeping on the right-hand sidewalk.

CHARLESTOWN VIEWED FROM COPP'S HILL IN THE 1830s.
NOTE THE UNFINISHED MONUMENT JUST RIGHT OF CENTER.

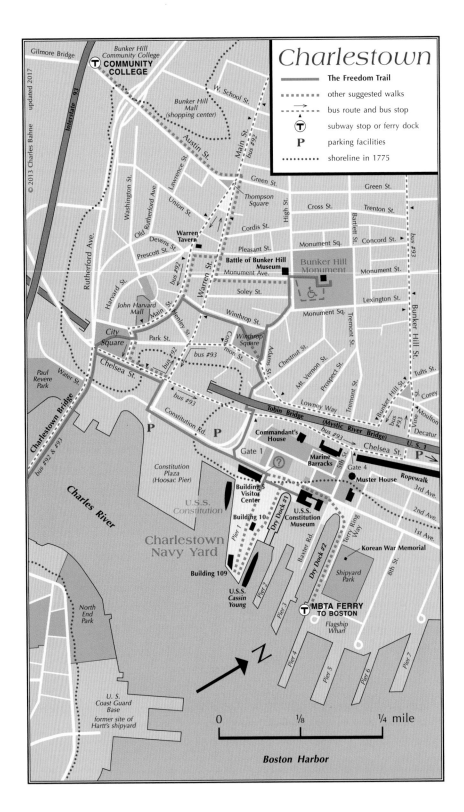

Charlestown

━━━━━	**The Freedom Trail**
∙∙∙∙∙∙∙∙	other suggested walks
– – –→	bus route and bus stop
Ⓣ	subway stop or ferry dock
P	parking facilities
∙∙∙∙∙∙∙∙	shoreline in 1775

Gilmore Bridge

Bunker Hill Community College

Ⓣ COMMUNITY COLLEGE

updated 2017

© 2013 Charles Bahne

Interstate 93

Bunker Hill Mall (shopping center)

W. School St.

Austin St.

Main St. bus #92

Green St.

Green St.

Thompson Square

Cross St.

Trenton St.

High St.

Bartlett St.

Concord St.

bus #93

Washington St.

Old Rutherford Ave.

Lawrence St.

Union St.

Cordis St.

Monument Sq.

Devens St.

Prescott St.

Pleasant St.

Warren Tavern

Battle of Bunker Hill Museum

Monument Ave.

Bunker Hill Monument

Monument St.

Rutherford Ave.

Harvard St.

Soley St.

Lexington St.

Monument Sq.

Tremont St.

Bunker Hill St.

John Harvard Mall

Main St.

Henley St.

Winthrop St.

Winthrop Square

Adams St.

Monument Sq.

Chestnut St.

Mt. Vernon St.

Prospect St.

Tremont St.

Tufts St.

City Square

Park St.

Common St.

Bunker Hill Ave. Corey

Moulton

Paul Revere Park

Water St.

Chelsea St.

bus #92

bus #93

bus #93

Lowney Way

bus #93

Decatur

Charlestown Bridge

bus #92 & #93

Constitution Rd.

Tobin Bridge (Mystic River Bridge)

bus #93

Chelsea St.

U.S. 1

P

Charles River

P

Constitution Plaza (Hoosac Pier)

P

Commandant's House

Gate 1

?

Marine Barracks

5th St.

Gate 4

Muster House

Ropewalk

3rd Ave.

2nd Ave.

1st Ave.

U.S.S. Constitution

Building 5 Visitor Center

Building 10

Pier 1

Dry Dock #1

U.S.S. Constitution Museum

Baxter Rd.

Terry Ring Way

Korean War Memorial

8th St.

Charlestown Navy Yard

Building 109

Pier 2

Dry Dock #2

Shipyard Park

North End Park

U.S.S. Cassin Young

Pier 3

Ⓣ **MBTA FERRY TO BOSTON**

Flagship Wharf

Pier 4

Pier 5

Pier 6

Pier 7

N

U. S. Coast Guard Base former site of Hartt's shipyard

0   ⅛   ¼ mile

Boston Harbor

The Freedom Trail – Charlestown

The Freedom Trail ends in Charlestown, across the river from downtown Boston. Once a separate community — and older than the city which has absorbed it — Charlestown has been "rediscovered" by new city dwellers after some years of decline.

A visit to Charlestown can be combined with the rest of the Freedom Trail, or it can be done on a separate day. Because of Constitution's *long waiting lines, be sure to allow plenty of time if you want to go aboard the ship.*

From Copp's Hill, *it's a twelve-minute walk — about six-tenths of a mile — to City Square, following the Freedom Trail's red line across the Charlestown Bridge. Directions from other parts of the city are given below:*

☞ **By sightseeing trolley tour:** Most trolley tours allow you to stay at the Navy Yard as long as you like, then board a later trolley to complete the tour. This way you can walk the Boston part of the Freedom Trail one day, then combine your Charlestown visit with a trolley tour on the second day of your visit.

☞ **By boat:** The nicest way to get to Charlestown is the MBTA's Charlestown Ferry from Long Wharf — located at the end of State Street, next to the Aquarium Blue Line station, and just two blocks from Quincy Market. Ferries sail from Boston on the hour and half-hour until 6:00 PM, with extra rush hour service. Cash fare is currently $3.70 (children under 12 free); daily and weekly T passes are accepted if they're on a "CharlieTicket" (and not a "CharlieCard"). From the Charlestown dock at Pier 4, it's a very short walk to the *Constitution*. Call 617-227-4321 for info.

☞ **By transit bus:** Board MBTA bus #93 ("Sullivan Square") on Congress Street in downtown Boston: it stops at State Street, opposite the Old State House; at North Street, by the Curley statue; and at Hanover Street, by the Haymarket subway station (Orange Line entrance). Buses run every 20 minutes Monday–Saturday, and every 45 minutes on Sunday afternoons. Get off on Chelsea Street, right outside Navy Yard Gate 1; from there you can also follow the Freedom Trail line to Bunker Hill. *The cash fare is presently $2.00 for adults, and free for children under 12 years old.*

☞ **On foot:** Allow half an hour to the Navy Yard from Faneuil Hall. Walk north on Congress Street. At New Sudbury Street, bear to the right, under the garage, and through the bus terminal. Then follow North Washington Street across the Charlestown Bridge. Be sure to stay on the right-hand (east) sidewalk on the bridge.

☞ **By subway:** *From downtown Boston, the ferry and bus are usually better choices than the subway.* **To the Navy Yard:** Take the Green or Orange Line to North Station; walk two blocks east on Causeway Street and turn left across the bridge, staying on the right-hand (east) sidewalk. **To Bunker Hill:** Take the Orange Line to Community College. You can see the monument from the station, which is six blocks away.

☞ **By car:** A public parking garage is on Constitution Road, just outside Gate 1, next to *Constitution*. Have your garage ticket stamped at the park Visitor Center and you'll get a reduced fee. Nearby streets have some metered parking. *If you park on the street, don't leave luggage or valuables where they can be seen inside your car.*

*Unless you come to Charlestown by boat, you'll probably arrive via the **Charlestown Bridge**. As you cross the bridge, notice the fine view of the Bunker Hill Monument ahead and to your right; then look further to your right down the Charles River, towards Boston Harbor. These waters, east of the bridge, are where Paul Revere rowed under* Somerset's *guns to start his midnight ride.*

In colonial days, a **ferry** crossed the Charles River here. The Boston Port Bill of 1774 — one of Parliament's "Intolerable Acts" — restricted the ferry and forced residents to make an 11½-mile overland detour. When the first Charles River Bridge opened in 1786, the 1,503-foot wooden span was claimed to be the longest bridge in the world. Among the investors in the privately-financed venture was John Hancock.

*At the foot of the bridge is **City Square**, the Puritans' first point of settlement in the Boston area in the 17th century.*

Once "trim and inviting in appearance", City Square has experienced many changes over the centuries. In the center of the square once stood the **Great House** where, on August 23, 1630, the Court of Assistants met to transfer the Massachusetts Bay Colony's government from Old World to New. Later known as the Three Cranes tavern, the building survived until the Battle of Bunker Hill in 1775. Portions of its foundation were uncovered during excavations for a highway tunnel in the 1980s, and some of the foundation stones have been placed on display in the park that marks the site today.

Called *Mishawum* by the Indians, Charlestown was first settled by Europeans in 1629. In that year, a small company of Puritans erected a fort and laid out streets in preparation for the "Great Migration" from England the following year. Both the town and its river were named in honor of King Charles, who had granted the colony its charter.

But the planners who chose this as the new colony's capital made one crucial mistake. The hundreds of Puritans who landed in "Charles Towne" during a midsummer heat wave in 1630 found the wells nearly dry and much of the available water brackish. As we have seen, most of the settlers soon crossed the river to Shawmut and its plentiful springs. Charlestown was essentially a sleepy country town until the Revolution.

Burned to the ground on June 17, 1775, the town was largely rebuilt by 1800. A second construction boom followed in the mid-1800s, when Charlestown became a "**streetcar suburb**" and was annexed by its larger neighbor. At this time, the Town gained its first Irish-blooded residents. They were "lace-curtain Irish", more well-to-do than their North End compatriots. To this day Charlestown has remained an Irish enclave.

Narrow Neck.   Bunker Hill.   Breed's Hill.   Moulton's Point.

VIEW OF CHARLESTOWN FROM BEACON HILL.

☞ *The Freedom Trail line comes to a fork at the foot of the Charlestown Bridge. You can visit U.S.S.* Constitution *first and then see Bunker Hill, or you can go first to Bunker Hill. This guidebook will take you first to the ship.*

(To see Bunker Hill first, cross Chelsea Street at the light, then follow the "Freedom Trail" signs through City Square Park. On the far side of the park, you'll rejoin the red line which leads to the monument.)

To go to **Constitution** *and the Navy Yard,* turn right at the end of the bridge onto Chelsea Street; after one block, turn right again onto Warren Street. Look for the steeple of Old North Church on the far side of the river; not far from here, Charlestown residents watched for Paul Revere's lanterns on the night of April 18, 1775.

At the foot of Warren Street, turn left onto Constitution Road. Follow the brick line as it goes straight into **Gate 1**, the Navy Yard's main entrance. Just inside the gate is a red brick building on the right side of the road. This is **Building 5**, which houses the **Navy Yard Visitor Center**. To enter, walk to the far end of the building and turn right.

☞ IMPORTANT NOTE: *To go in the Visitor Center, or to board* Constitution, *you must pass through a* **security checkpoint**. *Weapons and sharp objects are not allowed. You'll be asked to remove electronic items and metal objects from your pockets; all backpacks, purses, and wallets must be passed through an X-ray machine. Cameras and cell phones are permitted, and you don't have to remove your shoes.*

To board the ship, visitors over age 18 must also present a **photo ID** *(such as a passport or driver's license); but no* ID *is needed if you just want to go into the Visitor Center.*

U.S.S. Constitution

"Let us toast the ship! Never has she failed us!"

— *Commodore Bainbridge*

The most celebrated ship in American history is berthed here in the Charlestown Navy Yard, her home port for most of her life. One of the U. S. Navy's first vessels, U.S.S. *Constitution* was launched on October 21, 1797, to protect American merchant ships from depredations by Algerian pirates, and by the British and French navies. Invincible in war, this venerable ship has also survived numerous attempts at peacetime destruction. Now the oldest commissioned warship afloat in the world, the ship known as "Old Ironsides" has been the pride of our nation's naval heritage for over two centuries.

The act "to provide a naval armament", signed by President George Washington in 1794, authorized construction of six frigates in six different seaports. **Joshua Humphreys'** unusual design called for a ship larger and faster than a standard

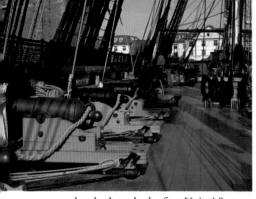

frigate, smaller and more maneuverable than a ship of the line. The result proved superior to anything else on the seas.

First known simply as "Frigate D", *Constitution* was built at Hartt's shipyard in Boston's North End, just across the Charles River from where she sits today. The work took three years and cost $302,718.84. She was the Navy's third vessel to be launched, after *United States* and *Constellation*.

Constitution was rated at 1,576 tons and 44 guns — although she usually mounted about 54 pieces of artillery — and carried a crew of 450 to 500 men, including 55 Marines and 30 "Boys". On her masts, a full set of 36 sails totaled nearly an acre of canvas.

Constitution's hull is built partly of **live oak**, its "durability being estimated at five times that of common white oak." This rare wood, from Georgia's sea islands, gave "Old Ironsides" her great strength. Cannonballs bounced off her nearly impenetrable hull and fell harmlessly into the sea.

During *Constitution*'s battle with *Guerrière* in 1812, an unnamed seaman cried out, "Huzzah! Her sides are made of iron! See where the shot fell out!" — thus coining a nickname which has stuck ever since.

Of course, she is *not* really made of iron, for metal-clad ships were not invented until many years later.

Although she went to sea in 1798, *Constitution* saw little action for five years. In 1803 she sailed to the Mediterranean Sea, where the Barbary corsairs were menacing American commerce. By subduing the "haughty tyrant of Tripoli" — a nation now known as Libya — Commodore Edward Preble won the frigate her first major victory.

"Old Ironsides'" greatest exploits came during the **War of 1812**. Early in the war, *Constitution* encountered H.M.S. *Guerrière* on Georges Bank, 700 miles due east of Boston. Within 35 minutes, this "noble frigate" had turned the British ship into "a perfect wreck". Her enemy "lay rolling like a log" and had to be burned and sunk on the spot.

Britons, who regarded their maritime superiority as "part of the law of nations", reacted first with disbelief and then with gloom. Capt. Isaac Hull's "fir-built frigate" had handed the Royal Navy a stunning defeat.

Just four months later the lesson was repeated. "On the 29th Dec...., about 10 leagues from the coast of Brazil, the *Constitution* fell in with and captured H.B.M. frigate *Java*, of 49 guns and manned with upwards of 400 men. The action continued one hour and 55 minutes, in which time the *Java* was made a complete wreck, having *her bowsprit, and every mast and spar shot out* of her." Like *Guerrière*, *Java* had to be destroyed at sea. This time, Capt. William Bainbridge was the hero who took the prize.

CONSTITUTION (right) DEFEATS *GUERRIÈRE* IN 1812.

Early in 1815 the "eagle of the seas" logged one last major battle. Although the peace treaty with Britain had been signed nearly two months earlier, the news had not yet reached the coast of Morocco. Outnumbered and outgunned, Capt. Charles Stewart defeated the British sloops *Cyane* and *Levant* and added another victory to *Constitution*'s logbook.

The frigate's other exploits in the war included several minor engagements as well as two daring cat-and-mouse escapes. In the war for "Free Trade & Sailors' Rights", the war that assured our lasting independence, this "glorious Yankee vessel" had humbled the proud flag of His Britannic Majesty's fleet.

But wooden ships, however strong, have only a finite lifespan. In 1830, a Boston newspaper reported that *Constitution* was unseaworthy and would be broken up. "Ay, tear her tattered ensign down!" wrote Oliver Wendell Holmes, then a Harvard student, in a poem published nationwide. The resulting outcry prompted Congress to appropriate funds to restore her.

Mid-19th-century technical advances, however, made the gallant ship obsolete for warfare; since then her role has largely been symbolic. As a goodwill ambassador, she sailed around the world in 1844–46 and was towed through the Panama Canal to visit U. S. Pacific ports in 1931–34.

But there have been darker days. In 1905, after years as a receiving vessel (a floating barracks), minus her masts and rigging, "Old Ironsides" was considered for target practice. Holmes' poem was dusted off, and popular emotion again saved her. Two decades later, schoolchildren across the country gave their pennies to help finance a full restoration. The most recent threat came in 1974, when the closing of the Navy Yard here spurred rumors that Boston's pride would become Philadelphia's newest attraction.

Yet she has endured. As her crew boasts today, she is Boston's only undefeated team, with 33 captures and not one loss in her lifetime career.

Perhaps the oddest of *Constitution*'s many stories concerns the Andrew Jackson **figurehead** mounted on her during the 1833 overhaul. New Englanders, who viewed "Old Ironsides" as one of their own, reacted with disgust, for President Jackson was distinctly unpopular here.

One local man, Samuel Dewey, took it on himself to rectify the matter. Under cover of a stormy night, Dewey hoisted himself up from a rowboat and decapitated the wooden figure of "Old Hickory". The severed head was displayed around the city in triumph, and then Dewey personally delivered it to officials in Washington. But no Middlesex County jury would ever convict him of his crime of disrespect, so Dewey escaped scot-free.

Finally recovered in 2011, Andrew Jackson's jaw can now be seen here in the U.S.S. Constitution Museum; but the upper half of his head is in New York.

After you pass through the security checkpoint, and go through the Visitor Center, you sometimes may have to wait in another line to board the ship. Visits to the ship are generally self-guided, but Navy personnel are on hand to answer your questions, and to offer occasional presentations about the "Old Ironsides".

Constitution today

Still an active commissioned ship in the United States Navy, "Old Ironsides" is a unique part of our national defense and our national heritage. Unvanquished in battle and preserved by popular mandate, this Fighting Frigate is now open to visitors throughout the year.

The guides who escort you are active-duty enlisted men and women, selected out of the ranks to be the Navy's ambassadors to the American people.

Below decks, all has been restored where 450 men and teenagers lived for months and years at sea in incredibly close quarters. Like them, you will clamber up and down steep stairs or "ladders", and duck your head under 5½-foot deck clearances. As a warship, *Constitution* was built for strength and speed, not for the comfort of the men who sailed aboard her.

At the stern, glassed-in "quarter galleries" contain the captain's quarters — and his private toilet. You may wonder about the lack of privacy, but miles of open ocean usually separated the ship from any Peeping Toms. And from his seat, the captain could observe the masts and rigging above.

From the pier, *Constitution* is a magnificent sight: as tall as a 15-story building, and nearly 300 feet long from the tip of her bowsprit to her taffrail. Everything about her is shipshape, from her rigging to the gilded "catsheads" at her bow, from which her anchors are hoisted. But

each fall, parts of her rigging are removed to prevent winter storm damage, so her masts reach their full height only from June to September.

In 1992–97, *Constitution* underwent a complete overhaul here in the Navy Yard. Bracing timbers known as diagonal riders, removed generations ago, were reinstalled to restore much of the hull's original strength. Yet only about twenty percent of her timbers are still original, for "Old Ironsides" has been rebuilt many times over the years.

Today *Constitution* usually makes several excursions into Boston Harbor each year, pushed by tugs. In commemoration of her 200th birthday, she set sail off the coast of Marblehead, Massachusetts, on July 21, 1997. Hoisting a partial set of six sails on her masts, she caught the rush of the wind in her rigging for the first time since 1881. A second voyage under sail followed in 2012, celebrating the bicentennial of her victory against *Guerrière*.

If you wuld like to learn more about this famous vessel, a visit to the **U.S.S. Constitution Museum** is in order. Here children and adults can learn about the men who built and commanded "Old Ironsides", the men (and youths) who actually lived, fought, and died on her decks.

The museum is in gray granite Building 22, across the pier from *Constitution*. There's no admission fee for families or individuals — although donations are encouraged — and no need to go through the ship's security checkpoint.

On display are artifacts from the frigate's long career, including pieces of her structure that have been removed and replaced in her many rebuildings. You can furl a sail and view a replica cross-section of her 21-inch-thick hull. Dynamic exhibits tell of the ship's many victories and voyages, and allow you to second-guess her captains' decisions. And if for some reason you can't take an in-person tour of the ship, be sure to see the museum's informative, large-screen **video presentation.**

Charlestown Navy Yard

"Serving the Fleet" for 174 years

For the better part of two centuries, the Charlestown Navy Yard serviced, supplied, and built the ships of the United States Navy. It was also a spawning ground for some of history's most significant advances in naval technology, such as ship-to-shore wireless telegraphy, sonar, and die-lock anchor chain.

In 1800 — just three years after *Constitution* was launched — the federal government purchased some 65 acres of land, known as **Moulton's Point**, for one of its first Navy Yards. This was already historic ground, for in 1775 His Majesty's troops landed here to begin their advance on Breed's and Bunker's Hills. Located at the confluence of two rivers, it was a natural site for a

deep-water port.

By the Civil War, the Yard had launched over a score of navy vessels and had pioneered such innovations as granite dry docks and steam-powered rope-making. With the Norfolk Navy Yard in Virginia, it was the most complete and active naval facility in the nation. But a post-bellum lull followed until the Yard was redeveloped after 1900.

Activity in the Navy Yard reached its greatest peak during **World War II**. Up to 50,000 workers — including 8,500 women — were carried on the payroll here and at the yard's annexes, working 6-day, 54-hour weeks to build, equip, and repair the Navy's fleet. The war years saw "Rosie the Riveter" and her male and female coworkers build 159 ships and repair another 3,260 here in Charlestown. In one year, 1943, 60 vessels were completed, more than in all the 140 years before the war began!

After the war, activity in the Yard focused on overhaul and upgrading of the fleet, including installation of sonar domes and conversion of the world's first guided missile destroyer.

In its 174-year history, the Navy Yard's original 65 acres grew into a 130-acre industrial complex of 86 buildings, more than 3½ million square feet of floor space. Sawpits, sail lofts, and shot parks gave way to machine shops, electronics labs, and traveling overhead cranes.

All of this came to an end in 1974, when President Richard M. Nixon ordered the Navy Yard closed. Many Bostonians still claim that the decision was made to spite Massachusetts, the only state to have voted against Nixon in 1972. Others contend that it was a necessary economy in an age of airborne, rather than seaborne, defense.

The question now remained: What do you do with a 130-acre, surplus Navy Yard? City officials decided to turn it into the nation's largest privately-financed historic rehabilitation project. In a $340,000,000 effort, the Yard's buildings have been recycled into virtually a new city of offices, stores, research facilities, and housing.

The southwesternmost part of the Navy Yard, meanwhile, has been preserved as a **national park**. Within its boundaries, exhibits and displays are offered, and two historic ships — *Constitution* and *Cassin Young* — are open for tours.

*SIDETRIP: To begin a **self-guided walking tour** of the Navy Yard, start in front of the Visitor Center building, just outside the entrance to the security checkpoint.*

Building 5, which houses the park's Visitor Center, was erected around 1816 as a warehouse and office. Later the building served as a museum and as the Officers' Club. Today its upper floors are quarters for Constitution's *crew. It stands near the site where Paul Revere and his friends landed their rowboat on the night of April 18, 1775, as Revere set off to warn the country of the redcoats' march.*

Now walk out to the end of Pier 1. In the middle of the pier is the red brick **Building 10**, *which was originally erected for storing pitch. In World War II, it was a battery-charging facility for submarines. Today it houses "Shipyard Galley", a snack bar which is open seasonally.*

At the end of the pier, gray wooden **Building 109** *was the pilot house; from its penthouse a waterfront manager directed ships' movements around the Yard.*

Pause at the end of the pier to enjoy the view of the Boston skyline across the harbor, with the spire of Old North Church dominating the North End in the foreground. Then turn left and walk over to the destroyer U.S.S. Cassin Young.

U.S.S. *Cassin Young* DD-793

A Fletcher class destroyer, U.S.S. *Cassin Young* recalls the tremendous activity in the Navy Yard during World War II. Although *Cassin Young* was built in San Pedro, California, fourteen other ships just like her were produced here in Charlestown in 1943–44. In size, crew staffing, and purpose, *Cassin Young* is very much a 20th-century counterpart of *Constitution*.

The vessel bears the name of U. S. Navy Captain Cassin Young, who served with honor at Pearl Harbor and died at Guadalcanal. Launched and commissioned late in 1943, *Cassin Young* saw heavy action in the South Pacific, including service at Iwo Jima and Okinawa. Twice she was struck by kamikazes. After peacetime service in the Atlantic, she was mothballed in 1960. She is now on loan from the Navy to the National Park Service.

Ranger-guided tours of *Cassin Young* are offered in warmer months; or you can visit her main deck on your own, weather permitting.

Keep to the right as you walk back up the pier, being sure to notice the colorful **safety shoe billboard** *just beyond the Shipyard Galley.*

Dry Dock No. 1

On the right side of the pier is Dry Dock 1, sometimes called the John Quincy Adams dry dock. The Navy's second dry dock to be placed in use, it missed the honor of being the first by just one week. *Constitution* was the first ship to enter it, in 1833, and also the last ship in under Navy control, in 1974. The dry dock's original 305-foot length has been extended twice, in 1856 and 1948. It was designed by Loammi Baldwin, a noted civil engineer, and is built of granite from nearby Quincy, Massachusetts.

At the harbor end of the dry dock is a hollow, floating door called a **caisson**. To let a ship enter, the dry dock is filled with water and the caisson towed aside. The ship is brought in, the caisson replaced and filled with water to make it sink, and the dry dock pumped out. Water pressure holds the caisson shut, just like a drain stopper in a bathtub. Wooden blocks, placed on the bottom before the ship enters, support the vessel. When work is done, the dry dock is flooded and the caisson removed.

Beyond the dry dock you can see two granite buildings designed by **Alexander Parris**, the architect of Boston's Faneuil Hall Market. As the Navy Yard architect for many years, Parris drew up plans for fourteen of the Yard's buildings. Building 22, now the Constitution Museum, was built in 1832 as the dry dock's first pump house. At right is Building 24, originally a carpenters' shop, which now serves as *Constitution*'s maintenance facility.

*Turn right on **First Avenue** past the Constitution Museum and the **Scale House**. The fence and gate mark the boundary between the National Park and the redevelopment part of the Navy Yard. The view down First Avenue gives an idea of the Yard's immense size.*

Look to your left for a view of some historic buildings, not open to the public.

The octagonal brick **muster house**, designed by Joseph Billings in 1852, was where the Yard's civilian employees reported for work — the 19th-century equivalent of a time clock station. Later it served as a telephone exchange, and as a hearing clinic for shipyard workers. Today it houses private offices.

Behind the muster house you can spy the low granite **ropewalk** building. From 1838 to 1955, this quarter-mile-long structure produced most of the cordage used in the U. S. Navy. On a lesser scale, ropemaking continued here until 1971. Before the invention of nylon, rope was made from fibers of the hemp plant — also known as marijuana. Empty for many years, the building is now being converted to apartments.

The white structure at the right of the muster house was once a bank branch where Navy employees could cash their paychecks. Later it was home to the **Boston Marine Society**, founded in 1742 by Boston sea captains to "make navigation more safe" and to aid distressed mariners and their families. Each member paid monthly dues into "The Box", whose proceeds benefited those affected by "adverse accidents". Today the Society continues both of these activities from another location, nearby in the Navy Yard.

*From the Scale House, retrace your steps along First Avenue past the Constitution Museum. Across the lawn to your right is the **Marine Barracks**, part of which dates to 1810. In the 19th century, Marines were troops trained in hand-to-hand and ground combat, but based aboard Navy ships.*

To finish the Navy Yard tour, walk towards the flagpole, looking across the green to the bow-fronted Commandant's House.

Commandant's House

Erected in 1805, this stately 20-room residence was home to the Navy Yard's 63 chief officers and their families. This "comfortable dwelling house" represents the elegant side of life in the Yard. Among the dignitaries who were entertained here were many heads of foreign states, five U. S. presidents, and the Marquis de Lafayette.

An 1823 remodeling gave the house its strange façade. The Commandant allegedly would not agree to a design, so the architect cried, in exasperation, "Well, then, what design would you have me make it!?" "My arse!" was the supposed reply, and so it was. Whether the story is true or not, the result did have an unflattering anatomical resemblance — which was originally even more pronounced.

*Now return to Building 5, past a row of early 19th-century **officers' quarters** on your right. This completes the tour of the Navy Yard.*

END OF SIDETRIP: We shall now proceed to the Freedom Trail's next and final stop, Bunker Hill, a seven-minute walk away in a residential section of Charlestown.

Leave the Yard through Gate 1, which is next to Building 5 and the Visitor Center — the same place you entered the Yard.

*Just outside the gate, you'll come to a fork in the Freedom Trail's red line. To go to Bunker Hill, take the **right fork** before you come to the bus and trolley loop. With the Navy Yard fence on your right, walk along Constitution Road to the traffic signal at the end of the street. Cross the busy Chelsea Street intersection at the light, then walk through the **underpass** beneath the adjacent highway.*

Keep walking straight along Chestnut Street, then take the first left onto Adams Street. Follow Adams Street for one short block, until you come to Common Street. Cross this street and go into the park.

As if by magic, you are in the middle of jewel-like **Winthrop Square**, also known as the "Training Field". Juxtaposed around the square are buildings from both of Charlestown's great times of growth, the post-Revolutionary period and the 19th-

century Victorian era. To your left on Common Street are two Federal-style structures, the rambling brown Salem Turnpike Hotel of circa 1810 and the yellow three-story Arnold House of 1805. At right, Adams Street is lined with Greek Revival and Italianate townhouses from Victorian times.

From this simple green, men and sometimes boys left to fight in the wars of 1775, 1812, and 1861; today, two monuments recall the ones who never returned. In the middle of the square, sculptor Martin Milmore's Soldiers' Monument honors the Town's Civil War dead. Nearby, at the gateway to the very battlefield on which they were slain, memorial tablets list the names of the 140 Americans who fell atop and around Breed's Hill on June 17, 1775.

Walk through the park, then turn right on Winthrop Street, curving uphill towards the Bunker Hill Monument. (Don't be confused by the red line coming in from the left; this is the direct route from City Square to Bunker Hill.)

At the top of the street, pause to enjoy the view; then follow the red brick line to your left, around Monument Square with its classic rowhouses.

*Before going up the hill, be sure to visit the National Park Service's **Battle of Bunker Hill Museum** in the old public library building on the left side of the street, just beyond Monument Avenue. This free museum features dioramas and other displays about the battle, plus restrooms and a bookstore.*

*Now cross the street and climb the stairs. At the top is sculptor William W. Story's **statue of Colonel William Prescott**, commander of the American forces at the battle.*

Bunker Hill

"Don't fire 'til you see the whites of their eyes!"
— Col. Prescott's orders

"It was the first great battle of the Revolution," said Daniel Webster, many years later; "and not only the first blow, but the blow which determined the contest.... When the sun of that day went down, the event of independence was no longer doubtful."

Even Maj. Gen. John Burgoyne of His Majesty's Army seemed to agree. "Perhaps," he speculated, "a defeat was a final blow to the British empire in America."

Since the action at Lexington and Concord in April, the country had been preparing for war. Recruits for the new "New-England Army" poured into Cambridge, while British reinforcements arrived in Boston. Yet except for one skirmish and some peacock-like parading, nothing happened for almost two months.

Not that things were stable. British-held Boston was surrounded on all sides by "rebel" ground. High hills overlooked the city from both north and south; whoever controlled these hills would command the harbor. Did either side dare to mount an offensive?

"Gentleman Johnny" Burgoyne, the most eloquent and outspoken of Gage's generals, was eager to move. "What!" he exclaimed. "Ten thousand peasants keep 5,000 of the King's troops shut up! Well, let us get in and we'll soon find some elbow room!"

Gage's Council of War drafted the first plans. Their army would land on Dorchester Neck, south of Boston, and sweep around the capital in a broad arc. "The operations must have been very easy" — or so they thought. They were to be executed on Sunday, the 18th of June.

Just as at Lexington and Concord, American intelligence learned of Gage's plans in time to thwart them. This time, the patriot commanders decided on preemptive action — to "erect some Fortifications upon said [Bunkers-Hill], & defeat this design of our enemies."

So, on the night of June 16, 1775, "about a thousand" New England soldiers marched to Charlestown. "By the dawn of the day, they had thrown up a small Redoubt [a fortification of earth and timber], about 8 Rods [132 feet] square" atop **Breed's Hill** — not Bunker Hill. A last-minute change in the New Englanders' plans causes confusion even today about the battle's name.

The American works, a "sudden and unexpected" affair, caused astonishment when the redcoats spied them at daybreak. Still, His Majesty's generals had little respect for the Yankee "rabble". Those raw recruits would be no match for the Empire's finest soldiers. Taking the hill would be easy — so easy, thought Gage, that why not continue the planned sweep through the countryside? Charlestown would be only the first town to fall.

The British troops thus waited until afternoon to attack. Morning was spent baking bread and cooking meat for a three-day expedition.

It was a mistake. As General Burgoyne noted later, "every hour gave them [the rebels] fresh strength." By 2:00 PM, when the British rowed across the harbor, the Americans had thoroughly entrenched themselves atop the hill.

"And now," wrote Burgoyne, "ensued one of the greatest scenes of war that can be conceived."

British troops made three assaults on the American works that June 17. The first two offensives were nearly identical: Redcoats converged on the New Englanders' lines from three sides, marching in row upon orderly row in spite of the many fences and stone walls that lay hidden in the tall grass. Inside their woolen coats, His Majesty's men sweated under the sun of an 80°F day. On his back, each man carried blankets, rations, and equipment for a three-day march, a total load of 125 pounds. And on the front of each scarlet uniform was a white cross, a perfect target for the rebel marksmen.

To conserve precious gunpowder, the Americans had orders not to fire "'til you see the whites of their eyes" — orders which proved to be a stroke of genius.

The British regulars advanced further and further up the hill, meeting no re-

sponse. Were the rebels cowards? Were they even there? Why did they not fire?

The Americans waited still. Then, suddenly: "Fire!!"

Row after row of redcoats fell, mowed down by the patriots' guns. Some units lost three-quarters, even 90 percent of their men. Casualties were greatest among the officers, who were singled out by the provincials as targets.

Only by "useing the most passionate gestures, & pushing the men forward with their swords" did the surviving British officers convince their men to march again.

A second assault, half an hour later, had much the same result.

It was the third attack, an hour after the first, which was the "decisive effort". Artillery fire and fresh reinforcements joined the British fight; the heavy knapsacks were left behind.

Since snipers firing from Charlestown village were harassing his troops, General Howe ordered the town burned. Red-hot cannonballs launched from Copp's Hill turned "380 dwelling-houses and other buildings" into "one great blaze". So appalled was the Continental Congress at this act of destruction that it agreed to pay the town's residents £117,982 for their losses.

But the pivotal fact was that the Americans ran out of gunpowder.

Lacking both powder and bayonets, the patriots' cause was lost. The provincials valiantly held the royal troops off with hurled stones and "the Butt-ends of their Musquets". The New Englanders' retreat was orderly, but their casualties mounted because they could no longer fight back.

The most lamented of their losses was Maj. Gen. **Joseph Warren**, dead of a musket ball through his head at the edge of the redoubt. The beloved Dr. Warren — he was a medical doctor — had been an eloquent orator for the patriot cause. With Hancock and Adams away in Philadelphia, he was the colony's foremost remaining patriot. It had been Warren, President of the Committee of Safety, for example, who had sent his dear friend Paul Revere on that midnight ride just two months before. Commissioned a major general but still without specific orders, Dr. Warren had vol-

unteered to fight as a private in the thick of the battle.

Bunker Hill was technically a **British victory**, for Howe's men held the bloody summit when it was over. But the pride of the empire lay exhausted, wounded, dead, and dying. Their planned foray around the bay was forgotten, not just for one day, but forever.

Publicly, General Gage called it "a complete victory"; privately, he admitted that "The loss we have sustained is greater than we can bear." His tally showed 1,054 of his men killed or wounded, nearly half of those who fought. On the other side, the American casualties were only 441 men from a much larger force.

Patriot General Nathanael Greene summed it up well: "I wish," he said, "I could sell them another hill at the same price."

Bunker Hill Monument

The prim urban park you see today bears little resemblance to the expanse of pasture that patriots and redcoats viewed in 1775. It is difficult to remember that this was indeed a battlefield, the very parcel of land on which the opposing armies fought on that bloody June 17.

Or at least part of a battlefield. The Bunker Hill Monument Association — the private group that built this imposing monument in 1825–42 — originally hoped to save all of the battleground. But the cost of erecting the granite shaft proved too high, and most of the land had to be sold to pay for it. Fine townhouses now surround Monument Square instead.

The cornerstone was laid by Lafayette, on the 50th anniversary of the battle, June 17, 1825. Daniel Webster was orator that day, as he was again at the dedication in 1843. The 17½-year construction period was due largely to a lack of money. Just as bake sales today finance many a project, so "the mothers and the daughters" of Boston held a fair at Faneuil Hall Market in 1840, and raised $30,035 to help complete the monument.

The final $10,000 donation, for the capstone, was from Judah Touro, a Jewish philanthropist who had once lived in Boston.

Architect **Solomon Willard**'s design was judged the best proposal, for which he was awarded $100. The 221-foot granite obelisk was one of the earliest examples of the Egyptian Revival style of architecture. It was also a tremendous engineering feat

Bunker Hill Monument, Boston, Mass.

for its day. The nation's first commercial railroad was built in Quincy, Massachusetts, just to haul the stone blocks from the quarry to a waterside dock. Nothing so grand had ever been accomplished in America; and it was not surpassed until the Washington Monument, 2½ times as high, was completed 40 years later.

At the base of the monument is the **lodge**, where are displayed statues of the battle's immortal heroes. Also inside is an information desk, where park rangers can answer your questions about the historic battle.

Atop the shaft is an **observatory**, from which "there is a magnificent view of the city, the harbor, the surrounding towns, and the outlying country stretching far into the distance." But only the hardy of health should attempt the climb: there are 294 steps, and no elevator!

Even if you do not climb the monument's spiral stairs, there is much to see from the summit of the hill. Turn left as you come out of the lodge, and pause at the top of the stairs; a stone marker on the ground near here indicates a corner of the Patriots' fortification on that historic day. Then look ahead in the distance, past the townhouses that now line the square.

North of the Town, an industrial area on the banks of the Mystic River is sometimes visible through the trees. On June 17, 1775, a **breastwork** "nearly 400 feet in length" extended towards the river. Beyond this, and to your left, was the **rail fence** at the river's shore, where Colonel Stark and his men from New Hampshire held off the royal grenadiers in some of the bloodiest action of the day.

Then look to your left for the old high school building, now converted to residences. Just to the right of that, look for the **steeple** of St. Francis de Sales Church in the distance. This granite church stands atop the true **Bunker Hill**. The monument here rises over the hill where the American fort was built: **Breed's Hill**. Breed's Hill was only half as high as Bunker Hill, but it was closer to Boston and presented more of a threat to royal rule. It was also less defensible.

Colonel Prescott, ordered to fortify Bunker Hill, decided instead to erect the redoubt atop Breed's Hill when he arrived in Charlestown late at night. But the fight has always been known as the "Battle of Bunker Hill".

Besides Prescott's change in plans, there are two other reasons for the name confusion: One, the name of Breed's Hill was not generally known beyond Charlestown, while Bunker Hill was a prominent landmark; and, two, Lieutenant Page, a mapmaker with His Majesty's Engineers, reversed the two names on the official plan of the battle which he sent to London. Some other maps showed just one hill.

There was, in short, as much confusion about the name of the hill in 1775 as there is today!

☞ *Bunker Hill is the last official Freedom Trail site — but you'll need to get back to Boston.* **The route described below does not follow the red line,** *but it passes by a number of important historical sites en route to nearby transit stops.*

Go down the stairs by Colonel Prescott's statue; then leave the monument grounds through the Massachusetts Gate — where you came in — and walk back towards the Museum building.

*Now walk straight down **Monument Avenue**, next to the museum. Laid out in the mid-1800s, this is Charlestown's finest street. At the bottom of the hill, turn right on Warren Street for one short block; then stop at the corner of Pleasant Street.*

To your left on Pleasant Street is Charlestown's most historic building, the **Warren Tavern**. Built before 1780 by Captain Eliphelet Newell, this was one of the first structures erected after the Town was burnt by British fire. It was named in

honor of the patriot General Joseph Warren, who died, as we just saw, at Bunker Hill. President Washington stopped here for "refreshments" in 1789; five years later the tavern became headquarters of Charlestown's first Masonic lodge. Paul Revere, a charter member and later grandmaster of that King Solomon Lodge, termed it "my favorite place". Restored in 1971, the tavern is open daily for food and drink.

Nearby are several Federal-period houses which have been restored, and even a few new houses built to resemble older ones.

☞ *To return to Boston by subway, continue northwest on Warren Street to the first stoplight, which is Thompson Square. Turn left on Austin Street, past a shopping center and across busy Rutherford Avenue. Community College* MBTA *station (Orange Line) will be on your right, about 4/10 of a mile from here.*

☞ *To go to Boston by foot, ferry, trolley, or bus, or to return to the Navy Yard, turn left on Pleasant Street, walk past the Warren Tavern, and turn left again on* **Main Street**, *which will take you past some more historic sites.*

Just across Main Street is the splitstone **Austin Block**, built circa 1822 for General Nathaniel Austin, the county sheriff. Its unusual walls are made of stones found on Outer Brewster Island in Boston Harbor.

At the corner of Monument Avenue stands the John Hurd house of 1795. For many years it housed a drugstore, and it still sports stained glass windows from its pharmacy days. Just beyond Hurd's house, the tan wooden house at 55 Main Street was the post-Revolutionary home of **Deacon John Larkin**, the man who lent Paul Revere his horse. Years later, Larkin reminisced about the "very good" horse, probably the best one in Charlestown, that was taken prisoner by a British patrol on that historic night.

At Winthrop Street you'll rejoin the Freedom Trail's red brick line. Continue southeast on Main Street, following the Trail until you come back to City Square.

Town Hill, the neighborhood adjacent to City Square, is the oldest part of Charlestown, dating back to the first few settlers who arrived in 1629. All traces of that early settlement were destroyed by the British in 1775.

The plaza surrounded by a brick wall on the right side of Main Street is the **John Harvard Mall**. This park was laid out in the 1940s in honor of John Harvard, a "sometime minister of God's word" who lived nearby. When Harvard died in 1638, he left his library and half his money — some 320 books and more than £800 — to the still-unnamed college at Cambridge. In return for this generous bequest (about $140,000 in today's money), it was ordered that the college "shalbee called Harvard College." Contrary to popular belief, John Harvard was not the college's founder, nor did he have any association with the school until he was on his deathbed.

Along the walls of the Mall are numerous historical plaques, which tell of the early settlement.

You've reached the end of the Freedom Trail. Congratulations!

From here you can return to the Navy Yard or go back to downtown Boston. No matter what your destination, follow City Square around to your left, past the yellow brick Roughan Hall building, toward Chelsea Street.

☞ **To walk back to Boston,** *follow the red line across the street into City Square Park; walk through the park and over the Charlestown Bridge. The most direct route to* **Faneuil Hall** *is North Washington Street, which leads straight on the far side of the bridge. For* **North Station,** *turn right on Causeway Street just after the bridge.*

☞ **To take a transit bus to downtown,** *leave the red line and bear left towards busy Chelsea Street; then turn left and look for the bus stop. The bus will drop you off at the Old State House, among other stops. Buses operate every 20 minutes Monday–Saturday, and every 40–45 minutes on Sunday; the cash fare is $2.00.*

☞ **To return to the Navy Yard,** *turn left on Chelsea Street, then right at the next corner onto Warren Street. On the far side of Chelsea Street, you'll rejoin the red brick line. Turn left on Constitution Road, and follow the Trail to* **Gate 1.**

☞ **To reboard your sightseeing trolley tour,** *go back to the Navy Yard. The trolley stop is in the driveway just outside Gate 1.*

☞ **The ferry to Boston** *is the nicest way to return to Faneuil Hall or the Aquarium. The boat leaves from* **Pier 4** *in the Navy Yard: go to Gate 1, then walk straight through the Yard, past the U.S.S. Constitution Museum and the Scale House. After you pass the inlet of water, turn right on Terry Ring Way and walk out to the end of the pier. Boats sail from Charlestown at :15 and :45 past the hour, every day until 6:15 PM. On weekdays there's extra rush hour service, with the last boat at 8:15 PM. The cash fare is $3.70 (children under 12 free). Daily and weekly T passes are accepted if they're on a "CharlieTicket" (and not a "CharlieCard").*

About the author...

A Midwesterner by birth, Charles Bahne fell in love with Boston when he came here for college. After majoring in Urban Studies and Planning, he found a career in history and tourism, including three years as a ranger at Boston National Historical Park. As a tour guide and lecturer, he leads several programs a year for Road Scholar (formerly known as Elderhostel), and is available for other tours and programs. Besides this book, he's also the author of Chronicles of Old Boston, *published by Museyon Guides (2012). Contact him at newtownepub@yahoo.com.*

For general Boston tourism information:
Greater Boston Convention & Visitors Bureau ....www.bostonusa.com
Massachusetts Office of Travel & Tourism............................www.massvacation.com
Harborfest (activities during July 4 week) ....www.bostonharborfest.com
Massachusetts Bay Transportation Authority (trains, buses, ferries)......www.mbta.com

Websites about the Freedom Trail in general:
Boston National Historical Park..www.nps.gov/bost
Freedom Trail Foundation..www.thefreedomtrail.org
Scouts USA (Boy Scouts) Patch ....www.newenglandbasecamp.org/freedom-trail
Girl Scouts Patch..........................www.gsema.org; *enter "Freedom Trail" in search box*

Historic sites along the Freedom Trail (official trail sites are in bold type):
Boston Common ....www.boston.gov/parks/boston-common
Massachusetts State House ....www.sec.state.ma.us/trs
Beacon Hill neighborhood ...www.beaconhillonline.com *and* www.beacon-hill-boston.com
Black Heritage Trail.......................................www.maah.org/boston_heritage_trail
and ....www.nps.gov/boaf
Park Street Church ....www.parkstreet.org
Historic Burying Grounds..www.boston.gov/education/historic-burying-grounds-initiative
King's Chapel..www.kings-chapel.org
Boston Latin School ....www.bls.org; *click on "History" under "About BLS"*
Old City Hall ....www.oldcityhall.com
Old Corner Book Store ....historicboston.org/about *and* historicboston.org/ar
Boston Irish Famine Memorial..archive.boston.com/famine
Old South Meeting-House ....www.oldsouthmeetinghouse.org *or* www.osmh.org
Old State House..www.bostonhistory.org
Boston Massacre.............www.bostonhistory.org/bots-blog/2017/1/17/the-boston-massacre
and ....www.masshist.org/features/massacre
Boston Tea Party Ships and Museum..........................www.bostonteapartyship.com
Faneuil Hall...go.nps.gov/fh
Ancient & Honorable Artillery Company ....www.ahac.us.com
Printing Office of Edes & Gill...bostongazette.org
Faneuil Hall Marketplace ....www.faneuilhallmarketplace.com
New England Holocaust Memorial..www.nehm.org
Union Oyster House ....www.unionoysterhouse.com
North End neighborhood.........www.northendboston.com *and* www.north-end-boston.com
Paul Revere House ....www.paulreverehouse.org
"Paul Revere's Ride" (the poem) ....www.paulreveresride.org
Captain Jackson's Chocolate Shop (Clough House)....oldnorth.com/captainjacksons
Old North Church ....www.oldnorth.com
U.S.S. Constitution ....www.navy.mil/local/constitution
Naval Heritage Center........www.history.navy.mil; *click on "Learn About the Ship of State"*
U.S.S. Constitution Museum.....www.ussconstitutionmuseum.org *or* www.usscm.org
Charlestown Navy Yard..go.nps.gov/cny
and ....www.friendscny.org
U.S.S. *Cassin Young* ....www.nps.gov/bost/learn/historyculture/usscassinyoung.htm
Commandant's House ....www.nps.gov/bost/learn/historyculture/commandants-house.htm
Bunker Hill ....go.nps.gov/bh
and...www.nps.gov/bost/planyourvisit/bhm.htm
Battle of Bunker Hill Museum ......www.nps.gov/bost/learn/historyculture/bhmuseum.htm
Warren Tavern ....www.warrentavern.com

And for "history, analysis, and unabashed gossip about the start of the Revolution":
J. L. Bell's "Boston 1775" blog...www.boston1775.net

Boston Common Visitor Center – Fully accessible including **restrooms**.

Faneuil Hall Visitor Center – Fully accessible including **restrooms**; elevator to all floors. Use ramped entrance on the south side of the building, near the Bostix ticket booth.

Navy Yard Visitor Center – Fully accessible including **restrooms**.

Boston Common – Fully accessible, except for steps at the Beacon Street entrances.

Massachusetts State House – Most of building is accessible by elevator. Ground-level entrance is on Bowdoin Street side of building (around the corner, to right of the main entrance).

Park Street Church – Elevator available. Send a friend into the main entrance to alert the staff, or go to the church office at 1 Park Street (new building next to church).

Granary Burial Ground – Ground-level entrance at the end of Tremont Place. Follow the Trail past the burial ground gate; turn left on Beacon Street and left again into the first alley; walk to end of alley and go through gate on the right.

King's Chapel – One 2½″ sill at entrance gate; ground floor is otherwise fully accessible.

King's Chapel Burial Ground – Entirely at ground level, but be careful of uneven paths.

Old South Meeting-House – Ramp located on north (left) side of the church tower and the main entrance. Fully accessible including **restrooms**; elevator to all floors.

Old State House – Eight 8″ steps and narrow doorways at entrance, plus additional steps to some exhibit areas. Accessibility improvements for this historic building are being planned.

Boston Tea Party Ships – Fully accessible including **restrooms**, except that below-decks areas of the ships are accessed only by stairs. Elevator to all floors of the museum building.

Faneuil Hall – Use ramped entrance on the south side of the building, near the Bostix ticket booth. Elevator to all floors; accessible **restrooms** on second floor and in basement.

Faneuil Hall Marketplace – Most areas are accessible by ramps and elevators, except for some stores in basements. **Restrooms** are in the basement of the Quincy Market building, and are accessible by elevator from the main food hall (ramp up from ground level).

Haymarket – Wheelchair users should avoid this area if possible on Fridays and Saturdays due to extreme congestion.

North End – Curb cuts and sometimes entire sidewalks may be blocked by parked cars; sidewalks are often too narrow for wheelchairs. Some creative route-finding may be necessary.

Paul Revere House – Fully accessible by ramps and an elevator, including **restrooms** in the Education and Visitor Center building.

St. Stephen's Church – Three 6″ steps at entrance.

Clough House – One 2½″ sill at entrance. All facilities and exhibits are on one level, but narrow doorways may impede access.

Old North Church – One ½″ sill at entrance. Gift shop is in a separate building: seven 7½″ steps at entrance; four additional steps up to some merchandise at the rear of the store. The crypt and the tower, included in the "Behind the Scenes" tour, are accessible only by stairs.

Copp's Hill Burying Ground – Six 8½″ steps at entrance. To view burying ground from street, use Charter Street (one block north of Old North Church), but no entry on that side.

U.S.S. *Constitution* – Ramped gangplank and steps up to main deck; slope of tamp and height of steps will vary with tide conditions. Navy personnel may be able to assist. Access to below decks is only by steep stairs. Strollers are not permitted on board the ship.

U.S.S. Constitution Museum – Ramp located on left side of main entrance steps. Fully accessible including **restrooms**, with elevator to second floor.

U.S.S. *Cassin Young* – Eight 7½″ steps at entrance. Access to below decks only by stairs.

Bunker Hill Monument – Curbside parking available, or use curb cut at south corner of grounds (facing Winthrop Street). The ramp to top of hill starts on the southeast side, opposite Monument Avenue and the Bunker Hill Museum. The entrance into the lodge (on the left side of the building) is ramped. The monument has 294 steps to the top; no elevator.

Battle of Bunker Hill Museum – Fully accessible including **restrooms**; elevator to all floors.